INTERMARRIED COUPLES
IN THERAPY

ABOUT THE AUTHOR

Man Keung Ho (Ph.D., Florida State University) is Professor of Social Work at the University of Oklahoma. He is presently Director of the Norman Transcultural Family Institute and an External Examiner for the Chinese University of Hong Kong. A clinical member and Approved Supervisor of the American Association for Marriage and Family Therapy, he has published over 70 articles and several books on marriage and family therapy, including *Building a Successful Intermarriage* (1984) and *Family Therapy with Ethnic Minorities* (1987). In addition, he is serving on several editorial boards, including *Journal of Multicultural Social Work, Journal of Marital and Family Therapy,* and *Journal of Education for Social Work.*

INTERMARRIED COUPLES IN THERAPY

By

MAN KEUNG HO, Ph.D.

CHARLES C THOMAS • PUBLISHER
Springfield • Illinois • U.S.A.

l Throughout the World by

CHARLES C THOMAS • PUBLISHER
2600 South First Street
Springfield, Illinois 62794-9265

© *1990 by* CHARLES C THOMAS • PUBLISHER

ISBN 0-398-05652-8

Library of Congress Catalog Card Number: 89-20462

With **THOMAS BOOKS** *careful attention is given to all details of manufacturing and design. It is the Publisher's desire to present books that are satisfactory as to their physical qualities and artistic possibilities and appropriate for their particular use.* **THOMAS BOOKS** *will be true to those laws of quality that assure a good name and good will.*

Printed in the United States of America
SC-R-3

Library of Congress Cataloging-in-Publication Data

Ho, Man Keung.
    Intermarried couples in therapy / by Man Keung Ho.
      p. cm.
    Includes bibliographical references.
    ISBN 0-398-05652-8
    1. Marital psychotherapy. 2. Interracial marriage—Psychological
aspects. I. Title.
RC488.5.H59 1990
616.89'156—dc20   89-20462
                                 CIP

PREFACE

Recent political and social changes in the United States have brought together people of diverse racial, national, and ethnic backgrounds. The civil rights movement of the 1960s broke down many of the barriers which, in the past, had kept Whites and Blacks apart. People of all ages are in contact with different races, nationalities, and ethnicities in schools and colleges, on jobs, through integrated housing, and in recreational and cultural activities. They participate together in business, politics, and social movements. The sharing of common tasks and goals in the Peace Corps and VISTA, the United State's military involvement in other countries, fellowships to study abroad, and liberal immigration laws all foster contact among individuals of diverse backgrounds. For many this contact has resulted in attachments, deep interpersonal relationships, and eventually intermarriage.

The term intermarriage generally refers to a marriage in which the parties' racial, ethnic, nationality, or religious backgrounds differ. This book excludes interreligious or interfaith marriage, although such exclusion by no means implies that interfaith marriage is not important or problem-free. Actually, it has become a common form of intermarriage that deserves separate and wider attention than can be provided here. Hence, intermarriage in this book refers specifically to *interracial* or *interethnic* marriage. Examples of the former include a Black, Hispanic, American Indian, or Asian married to a White person or a Black person married to an Asian person. Examples of interethnic marriage include an Irish married to an Italian, or a Japanese married to a Chinese.

This book focuses on interracial and interethnic marriages for five important reasons. First, these marriages represent the greatest cultural, political, social, religious, and language differences which make marital harmony difficult. Second, interracial couples are most vulnerable to alienation from both racial groups for their union and may thus be forced into couple isolation. Further, their children often experience great difficulty in establishing a clear identity and may be subjected to discrimination from both families in addition to discrimination from the mainstream societal group. Third, interethnic marriage, in addition to being demographically the most common form of all intermarriage (Crester and Leon, 1982; Leslie, 1982), deeply involves the couple's ethnic patterns of thinking, feeling, and behaving in both obvious and subtle ways. Ethnicity, defined as "those who conceive of themselves as alike by virtue of their common ancestry, real or fictitious, and who are so regarded by others" (Giordano, 1977), plays a vital role in determining what and how each spouse eats, works, relaxes, celebrates holidays and rituals, and how each spouse feels about life, death, and illness. Fourth, a vast majority of interracial marriages involve a White person and a person of color who usually is a member of an ethnic minority (Black, American Indian, Asian American, or Hispanic) and may feel discriminated against. Marital therapy for such couples requires a transcultural framework which takes into consideration the reality of both races. Fifth, there is evidence that ethnic minority groups have long been underutilizing mental health and counseling services (Jones, 1977; Fujii, 1976; Barrera, 1978). Ethnic minorities who intermarry seldom seek therapy for their problems (Ho, 1987; Ho, 1984). Their underutilization of therapy also is compounded by the fact that very few therapists are trained to provide transcultural therapy to intermarried couples.

Statistics indicate that interracial and interethnic marriages are increasing, although the exact number in the United States is difficult to ascertain. Among other factors, national data on intermarriage are unavailable because laws prohibit racial and ethnic identification in many public records. However, according to the 1980 census, in New York state alone, 34 percent of second-generation Puerto Rican men and 32 percent of second-generation Puerto Rican women, married and living with their spouses, are married to non-Puerto Ricans. Nationally, this is higher; 68 percent of second-generation Puerto Rican men and 65 percent of the women married and living with their spouses were married to non-Puerto Ricans. In Albuquerque, Los Angeles, and San Antonio, the latest available figures indicate as many as one in three Mexican Americans marries an Anglo (Alvirez et al., 1981).

The rate of intermarriage between Asian Americans and other races also shows rapid increase. Tinker (1972) completed a survey of the marriage records of Japanese Americans in Fresno, California, and found that 56 percent of the marriages were interracial. Urban associates (1974) found a high rate of intermarriage among other Asian/Pacific groups as well. The rise from under 10 percent in the 1950s to over 40 percent in the 1970s indicates the popularity of intermarriage with Chinese and other groups (Kitano and Yeung, 1982). Orthner and Bowen (1982) also report that the proportion of Asian-wife marriages at selective military installations in the Pacific ranges from one-quarter to one-half of all service marriages.

After laws forbidding interracial marriage were declared unconstitutional by a United States Supreme Court decision in June 1967, intermarriage between Blacks and Whites increased rapidly. In 1960, there were 51,409 Black-White marriages; in 1970, the total number of Black-White marriages had increased to 64,789 and by 1977, the number had increased to 125,000 (Bureau of the Census, 1978).

The extent of American Indian intermarriage is also reflected by Canadian Indian statistics (D.I.A.N.D., 1975) and by the Bureau of Indian Affairs (Jones, 1974). These indicate that despite the threat of loss of Indian status and government benefits, 29 percent of all those marrying are involved in intermarriage.

While interracial and interethnic marriages are increasing rapidly, little research has been devoted to this social reality and few studies explore its intricacies. Most literature on intermarriage has not advanced beyond theorizing from the point of view of sociology and anthropology (Crester et al., eds., 1982; Gordon, 1980; Porterfield, 1978; Stuart and Abt, eds., 1973; Tseng et al., eds., 1977). There are few publications that provide specific information for helping intermarried couples deal with their problems (Ho, 1984; McGoldrick and Garcia Preto, 1984). Resource material available for therapists is even more scattered. A majority of it focuses on an isolated segment of the intermarriage. **Family therapists and students need theory-based practical material that can help them in assisting couples involved in intermarriages. This book has been researched and written to meet that need.**

Seven important features frame the organization of this book: (1) It provides family therapists and students with an up-to-date resource of the realities and problems common in intermarriages (Chapter 1). (2) It delineates the cultural perspectives on problem-solving for the intermarried (Chapter 2). (3) It provides a transcultural, theoretical framework from which to derive appropriate assessment and therapeutic guidelines in therapy with intermarried couples (Chapter 3). (4) It provides a transcultural theory-based "how to," that is, specific information on transcultural relevant marital therapy models, strategies, skills, and techniques at the assessment and engagement stage (Chapter 4) and the problem-solving stage (Chapter 5). (5) Included are premarital therapy, divorce therapy, and therapy with the single-parent family and military family (Chapter 6). (6) It provides detailed case examples to illustrate the differential application of transcultural theory-based techniques and skills (Chapter 7). Two appendixes are provided: (A) Intermarriage Potentials Inventory, and (B) Ethnic Competence Inventory, to aid therapists who work specifically with the intermarrieds.

The content and the organization of this book can provide practitioners and students with a comprehensive, up-to-date examination of therapy with the intermarried. The book also provides an analytical and functional format that lends itself to the systematic ordering of information and a promising challenge of quality for transcultural therapy with this often overlooked, high-risk, but underserved population. Practicing family therapists will find that the book presents **practical** information and guidelines that they can readily use in their work with intermarried couples and families. In the academic arena, a specification of knowledge, techniques, and skills in intermarriage therapy should facilitate the learning process of both undergraduate and graduate students. An important new alternative to marital therapy with the intermarried is introduced that considers the cultural background of both the couple and the therapist.

It is generally recognized that there is not only considerable interracial and interethnic diversity, but that there is also marked and significant interracial and interethnic heterogeneity. In an attempt to delineate and systematize knowledge about marital therapy with intermarrieds, the possibility of stereotyping obviously is great. Aware of this danger, I have consulted extensively with a panel of distinguished practitioners who work closely with intermarried couples.

In order to present this book as a practice guide, its content has been infused with case examples covering the entire spectrum of marital problems faced daily by intermarried couples.

ACKNOWLEDGMENTS

I wish to thank the following people:

Leona Huffaker for editing an early draft of the manuscript.

Many intermarried couples represented in these pages who deserve my gratitude.

The secretarial staff of the Information Processing Center of the University of Oklahoma who typed the manuscript.

Professor Vickie Hill who read and critiqued parts of the manuscript.

My wife, Jeannie, who taught me the joy and wisdom of intermarriage.

My two sons, Christopher Yan-Tak and Stephen Yan-Mong, who excused me when I locked myself up in a library room to work and entertained me whenever I took a break from writing.

CONTENTS

INTERMARRIED COUPLES
IN THERAPY

PART I
CONCEPTUAL FRAMEWORK

Chapter 1

REALITY OF INTERMARRIAGE

Intermarriage, like any other marriage, is a continuous process in which two individuals learn to live together. They learn to adjust to each other in order to work toward common goals and achievements. When persons of different racial and ethnic backgrounds marry, their adjustment difficulties are likely to exceed those of couples with a common background. To the normal differences in personality, social class, education, and life experiences, couples of different ethnic and racial groups must add differences in values, customs, and traditions. The main objective of this chapter is to examine some of the problems that result from these differences and their relevance to the assessment phase of therapy with intermarried couples.

Generally, adjustment problems in racial and ethnic intermarriage can be traced to two major sources: (1) the ecological or person-in environment barriers or (2) the couple's interaction as husband and wife and as parents. The remainder of the chapter focuses on specific problems within those two major sources. Suggested guidelines for assessment and solutions to problems discussed here will be offered in Part II, "Techniques and Skills in Intermarriage Therapy."

ECOLOGICAL BARRIERS

Racism, Prejudice, and Discrimination

Racism and discrimination dominate the lives of many ethnic minorities and that, in turn, affects the adjustment of the intermarried. Racism, as is practiced in the unequal distribution of income, goods, and services among ethnic minorities, is made more obvious by the election in 1980 and 1984 of a U.S. president who reversed more than 50 years of development in social welfare. The socioeconomic status of many ethnic minorities, has actually degenerated.

Only 21 years ago, interracial marriages were still illegal in 16 American states. Mildred and Richard Loving married in Washington, D.C. in 1958 and returned to their rural home in Caroline County, Virginia, only to be awakened at two in the morning and carted off to jail by the county sheriff. "Almighty God created the races white, black, yellow, Malay and red, and He placed them on separate continents, and but for the interference with His arrangement there would be no cause for such marriages," wrote Loen M. Bazile, the judge who barred the Lovings from living in their home state. The black and white couple lived in "exile" in Washington for five years, but in 1963 they decided to return home and with help from the American Civil Liberties Union, fought the laws that deemed them criminals. In June 1967, the U.S. Supreme Court ruled miscegenation laws unconstitutional: Loving vs. Virginia became a milestone in the fight for the civil rights of interracial couples.

Society's aversion to interracial marriages may not be as much of a problem for couples as it used to be, but the struggle is far from over. Negative attitudes about miscegenation persist. As recently as 1983, the Texas Civil Liberties Union called for the removal of three justices of the peace who refused to perform interracial marriages. One of the justices, Eldon Scheffield of Tarrant County, openly echoed the pseudo-religious racism of Virginia Judge Leon Brazile: "If the good Lord had intended us to mix up like that he would have made us all the same color." As intermarried couples continue to struggle against racism, prejudice, and discrimination, their decisions about where to call home, for instance, are influenced not so much by laws anymore but by the knowledge that undisguised bigotry persists in many parts of the country. Intermarried couples can sense subtle discrimination by employers, real estate agents, and strangers. Some couples even endure rejection from their immediate and extended families. Such rejection can be in the form of financial loss and emotional support which the couples need desperately during family life cycle crises and transitions.

Social Class and Poverty

The median 1980 income for white families in the U.S. was $21,900; for minority families it was $13,470. Unemployment was a major factor that lowered the income level of minorities. From 1970 to 1981, the employment status of ethnic minorities increased from 8.2 to 14.3 percent; for whites the increase went from 4.5 to 6.9 percent (U.S. Bureau of the Census, 1981).

Social class refers to "differences on wealth, income, occupation, status, community power, group identification, level of consumption, and family background" (Duberman, 1975, p. 34). This definition is inadequate for a full appreciation of ethnic differences as they relate to intermarriage. A partner in intermarriage may act in accordance with his perceived class interest in some situations and in accordance with his cultural preference or minority identity in others. The term *ethclass* used by Gordon (1969) to describe the point at which social class and ethnic group membership intersect can serve as a useful guide in assessing how an intermarried couple interacts.

A limited number of ethnic minority members may have more income and be in the upper or middle class, work in more highly valued and rewarding occupations, and have more prestige than others. For a large number who are in the lower social class, the ethnic reality may translate into continuing discrimination in jobs, housing, education, health care, and social acceptance. Irregardless of one's present class, the influence exerted by the values that were acquired throughout childhood is often considerable (Mass, 1976). An individual's childhood value pattern is an adjustment reality and intermarried couples should be encouraged to assess its significance.

Immigration and Cultural Adjustment

The process of immigration necessitates voluminous life changes over a short period of time that are associated with lowered well-being (Holmes and Masada, 1974). There are two interrelated levels of adaptive cultural transition that every immigrant must face: (1) the physical or material, economic, educational, and language transitions, and (2) the cognitive, affective, and psychological transitions. These cultural transitions often cause dysfunction among immigrants, especially for intermarrieds from two different backgrounds.

Brislin (1981) postulated a set of principles that influence the cultural transition process: These principles can be useful in assessing an intermarried couple's adjustment. They include:

1. Attitude of the receiving host (friendly, hostile, or prejudiced).

2. Presence of other members of the same ethnic groups as family members, acquaintances, or friends.
3. Possession of marketable skills.
4. Knowledge of and familiarity with the host culture and its language.
5. Conditions of immigration, whether it was voluntary or compulsory.
6. Personality traits conducive to successful acculturation, such as the ability to develop interpersonal relationships, tolerance and flexibility in ambiguous situations, self-confidence and feelings of self-worth, and last but not least empathy.
7. Previous patterns in coping with crises and stressful conditions and the individual's coping defense mechanisms.
8. Similarity between the old and the new culture.

Three distinct coping strategies have been defined by Seelye and Wasilewski, (1979). They are (1) nonacceptance—behaving as if one were in the old culture; (2) substitution—behaving like people in the host culture; and (3) addition—behaving the old way with fellow nationals and behaving the new way with people from the host culture. Intermarried couples sometimes experience problems that can be attributed to an individual partner's cultural transition and the spouse's reaction to it. For the sake of marital adjustment, the immigrant spouse may need to adopt the "addition" strategy. At other times, the spouse from the host culture may need to understand and appreciate the partner's transitional difficulty and be willing to form a "third" culture characteristics of their marital situation.

Language and Physical Diversity

One of the unique problems encountered in intermarriage is the diversity of the language used by the couple. The language of both spouses conveys a wealth of information that can be classified as linguistic, ideosyncratic, or sociolinguistic (Ladefoged and Broadbent, 1957). Linguistic information is generally thought of in connection with language: it is the message that the speaker consciously attempts to communicate, the manifest content of the spoken word. Idiosyncratic information concerns inferences made from the quality of the speaker's voice and, by definition, derives from anatomical differences in the vocal tract. Speech not only communicates a message and information concerning vocal quality but also indicates a frame of reference, the context within which the message is interpreted and understood. Those contextual or socio-linguistic cues include information concerning the speaker's background, place of origin, group membership, status in the group, and relationship to the listener. This element of speech is acquired through the influence of the particular groups in which the speaker is or has been a member (Bryden, 1968). Ethnicity is experienced and persists through language. A common language provides a psychic bond, a uniqueness that signifies membership in a particular ethnic group. An intermarried couple with different native languages may have trouble sharing information, especially the sociolinguistic component. Even when one partner in the intermarriage is bilingual (and that bilingualism is a strong indicator of biculturalism), problems of miscommunication may still occur. A partner may not have acquired parallel vocabularies or may not know various meanings of words. Sometimes a person needs to use his native language to describe personal, intimate, or gut-level issues. A partner's lack of language skills can reinforce his or her low self-concept and status in the host community. Language difficulties can also make a person feel very defensive.

If the therapist can speak only English, the partner whose native language is not English will be placed in a severe disadvantaged position. A coalition, based upon similarity of spoken language between the therapist and the English speaking partner, can create an unsatisfactory triad. Furthermore, a spouse's use of nonstandard English can lead to a misdiagnosis and a distorted conceptualization of the marital conflict by the therapist. Hence, when presented with a client whose native language is different, the therapist should automatically assume that his or her judgement and objectivity are going to be compromised. The only questions that remain are how much and in what manner.

In-Laws and the Extended Family

Parents and relatives are a vital part of an individual's heritage. They form an individual's roots and significantly influence his future, including happiness in a marital relationship. The kinship bond an individual has with parents will always exist regardless of where a person resides, what he does, or how he feels about his parents. A positive relationship with parents and relatives provides an individual with a basic sense of belonging and security that helps that person form a satisfying and lasting marriage. Studies indicate that ethnic minority extended family ties are more cohesive and extensive than kinship relationships among the white population (Martin and Martin, 1978; Shimkin et al., 1978). An individual's relationship with his extended family may change after marriage, especially intermarriage. Factors that affect this change include the couple's motives for marrying, the family's injunctions or approval, or the new couple's distancing themselves from both extended families. Sometimes, one spouse may fuse into the other's family by religious conversion or by adopting the other's culture.

Choosing a partner from a different racial or ethnic group can allow a person to bring new possibilities into the family or to avoid interacting with the family by using the spouse as an excuse. At times one set of in-laws may be drawn into collusion with the couple against the other. The extended family may also stereotype the new spouse negatively. This is often a self-protective maneuver to reassure themselves when they feel that their son or daughter is rejecting them and their values by marrying out. At times parents' or relatives' negative reactions about intermarriage may derive from fears about being abandoned.

Due to cultural, racial, ethnic difference and sometimes geographic distance, it is rare for intermarried couples to remain open to *both* extended families and to keep their own cultural traditions, transforming them into new "culture" or patterns. A couple's accommodation to intermarriage may be easier in the short run if only one side of the extended family is available (Ho, 1984), since the couple will then have only one set of ongoing in-law relationships to handle. Serious loyalty conflicts may develop, however, on the part of the partner whose family is distant and not-available. This same partner is more likely to have difficulty adapting to later life-cycle transitions when most people feel a greater need for their cultural heritage. The difficulties inherent in these transitions tend to be more stressful when spouses are from different cultural backgrounds and nationalities and especially when they are without the support of their family of origin.

Adjustment to Family Life Cycles

The marriage relationship between a husband and wife is profoundly influenced by many forces that act upon them both as individuals and as a couple. The exact manner in which these forces affect them is determined by the present stage of their married life cycle. Generally, there are eight stages which every married couple experiences: (1) early marriage, (2) parenthood and early childhood, (3) middle childhood, (4) adolescence, (5) launching, (6) middle age, (7) preretirement, and (8) retirement and old age. These are not necessarily discrete life stages and often they overlap.

Racial and ethnic issues interact with the family life cycle at every stage of intermarriage. When this occurs, the stresses inherent in all change are compounded. As an individual goes through life cycle changes, he or she needs cultural identity most. Cultural identity provides the individual with the rituals, the symbols, and familiar meanings that cushion these changes. Any life cycle changes can trigger racial or ethnic identity conflicts, since it brings families closer to their roots. How the rituals are handled or celebrated may determine how well the couple or the family will adjust to the change (Friedman, 1980). All transitional and situational crises such as illness, job loss, retirement, children getting married, and death can compound racial and ethnic conflicts, causing the couple to lose a sense of who they are. Generally, the greater the cultural difference between the husband-wife, the more difficulty they will have understanding each other and adjusting to marriage. Their families will also have more trouble adjusting.

These barriers that result from racial, ethnic, and cultural differences are eternal to the intermarried couple's interactional relationship with each other. The following discussions will focus on the couple's interaction as husband and wife and potential problems they may encounter because of their racial ethnic and cultural differences.

SPOUSAL INTERACTION

Motivational Factors

By understanding the motives behind a couple's intermarriage, a therapist can identify their expectations of each other, confront their idealism with reality, strengthen their marital commitment, and assist them with problem-solving. There are numerous motivations for intermarriage, many of which are the same reasons for any marriage. Motivation for intermarriage can emanate from a combination of conscious and subconscious factors interacting at the same time (Cerroni-Long, 1985; Char, 1977). Generally, these are classified as sociological or psychological. Sociological motives are rooted in realities and time external to the individual and are usually beyond the individual's control. Psychological motives flow from one's intellect and emotions which govern the way one perceives, interprets, feels, and behaves toward others at a specific time and place.

Sociological motives for intermarriage include: chances and availability, financial security, social status, parental teaching, childhood rebellion, and stereotyped impression. Psychological factors that motivate couples to intermarry include: need to be different, act of aggression, sado-masochistic needs, oedipus complex, and superiority or inferiority complex.

In reviewing motives for intermarriage, one may form the opinion that most of the reasons listed so far have a negative connotation and that intermarried couples who possess these motives may have little chance for a successful marriage. This is seldom the case. A "correct" motive does not guarantee success in marriage. Motives for intermarriage represent past events for the married couple. Although motives have a heavy bearing on the outcome of a couple's present and future relationship, they are not the main determinants for a successful marriage. In reality, couples entering an intermarriage are motivated by a variety of reasons, not one single motive that fits into the neat sociological and psychological categories presented here. Additionally, different cultures and ethnic groups interpret motives differently. For example, due to cultural emphasis and ecological constraints, an ethnic minority is likely to place less emphasis on the romantic motive. Because of the collateral cultural value orientation, the same minority individual may feel less need to be different than Caucasians feel.

Food and Dining Etiquette

Different races and ethnicities have different eating habits, such as no pork or beef, fish on Friday, fasting on certain days, dietary observances during Lent, and the like. Such customs or requirements may not be a problem during courtship when romantic emotions run high and interaction between the couple usually is courteous and limited. They may loom as irreconcilable sore spots *after* the couple marries and begins to interact daily and intensely with each other. The following case example involving an interethnic couple illustrates this point.

On their one-month wedding anniversary Oi-ching, a Chinese wife, was upset when her Japanese husband, Yoko, prepared raw fish for the special celebration. After her initial shock and disbelief, Oi-Ching decided Yoko intentionally prepared raw fish as a means to express his resentment for having to cook for her that particular evening. In return, Yoko criticized Oi-Ching for being too provincial and refusing to try anything non-Chinese. As their argument progressed, Yoko criticized Oi-Ching for her bad table manners. He said that on several occasions she had used her own chopsticks to pass and serve food to their house guests. Oi-Ching was flabbergasted and explained that she used her own chopsticks to pass and serve food to family members and guests to demonstrate kindness, graciousness, intimacy, and respect. "How could it be?" responded Yoko. "The use of chopsticks to serve food is dirty and disrespectful. Chopsticks are frequently used to transfer the bones of the dead during Japanese funeral ceremonies and, therefore, should never be used to serve food to guests or family members in my house," added Yoko. The dietary and dining etiquette differences between Oi-Ching and Yoko clearly reflect their interethnic cultural backgrounds.

Festivities and Observances

Mike, a reformed Jew, and Mary, an Irish descendent, vowed that they would not allow their ethnic and religious differences to affect their marriage. Both are highly educated and successful professionals. Mike is an accountant and Mary is a registered nurse. They believed any problem could be overcome by reasonable discussion. To ensure their own individuality, they each have separate hobbies and a separate circle of friends in addition to their mutual friends. Mike occasionally attends synagogue, but Mary has not attended church for sometime because she usually works on Sundays. On special occasions, she attends synagogue with Mike.

A week before Christmas, Mary's brother brought her a Christmas tree, explaining that he happened to stumble on a good buy—two trees for the price of one. Mary placed the tree next to the fireplace in the family room and decorated it nicely. When Mike came home that evening, Mary jovially told him that the tree was a gift from her brother and that it reminded her of the warmth and pleasure of her childhood. Instead of sharing her excitement, Mike asked if he could move the tree from the family room to Mary's sewing room. Mary became annoyed and insisted that the Christmas tree was not meant as a religious symbol and that Mike should not be offended so easily and behave so immaturely. The couple did not speak to each other the rest of the evening. Next morning at breakfast, Mike finally broke the silence by relating to Mary the antisemitism which he had experienced as a child in a predominantly Christian neighborhood. Despite his constant struggle to keep things in proper perspective, the memories of harassment were still a vivid part of him. Consequently, Mike found Christmas a very taxing and uncomfortable time of the year. As Mike was expressing his feelings, Mary burst into tears. "As much as I sympathize with you and your Jewish experience, I find it difficult to give up part of me, for celebrating Christmas with the persons I love, apart from any religious implications. It has always been a warm and dear tradition for me," explained Mary.

Clearly, holidays and how they are observed vary among cultures. Couples contemplating intermarriage should be encouraged to discuss which holidays are important to each individual and how these days will be celebrated in the home and with family and friends.

Friendships and Social Network

An individual's sense of well-being does not occur in a social vacuum. An individual's ability to cope with daily stresses, critical life transitions, and environmental or cultural change, including intermarriage, is inextrically tied to the social ecology in which he or she is embedded. These "healing webs" (Pilisuk and Parks, 1986) or networks of social support have been the focus of extensive research, demonstrating the significance of informal relationships in dealing with uncertainty and marital life cycle change.

Intermarriage is a personal matter between two people whose continuing relationship and happiness depend also on their relationships with others. Through interacting with friends, the couple satisfies their social need for sharing and enrichment and avoids becoming too self-centered. Nevertheless, making friends and maintaining friendships present peculiar difficulties for many intermarried couples.

Nita, an American Indian, and Jerry, a Caucasian, had not socialized with friends for some time. Nita commented she was bored to death sitting at home doing nothing except complaining to Jerry that he shouldn't be watching television on weekends. Jerry replied that not leaving the house to socialize with friends was not his fault. If Nita's American Indian friends would accept him, he said he would be happy to go with her to visit them. "I always enjoyed visiting with friends before we married," added Jerry. Nita was curious about Jerry's comments regarding her Indian friends, and she asked if Jerry would elaborate on that statement. He explained that on numerous occasions when the couple had been out with Indian friends, they would stop laughing or talking every time he approached them. "They were not impolite or disrespectful to me, but they just stopped talking," added Jerry. "Interestingly enough, this is exactly how I feel when I am with your white friends," echoed Nita.

The couple's discomfort and their friends' discomfort are common problems for individuals when cultures, languages, and physical appearances are diverse. A couple's mutual understanding and acceptance of each other does not imply that their friends will be accepting. Friendship begins with common values, interests, and backgrounds. Friends of intermarrieds usually find that one partner in the marriage does not share their commonalities. Differences in background generate uncertainty, distrust, and discomfort, which restrict social relationships.

Some couples choose to relinquish their individual friends and make new friends with whom they feel compatible as a couple. This arrangement works only if the couple can agree on the meaning of compatibility. Also, the friends the couple selects must want to reciprocate friendship. This is not always the case, due to diverse cultural and ethnic backgrounds. The intermarried couple's difficulty in making and maintaining friendships also affects their leisure-time recreation and activities. Their isolation from friends forces them to interact more with each other and to depend more on each other for recreation and enjoyment. Thus, the couple's relationship may become too close, leaving no space for individuality and creativity. Soon, both parties in such a situation may feel stifled and begin to resent the constant presence of the other.

Financial Management

Money is a major problem area in many marriages, and especially in intermarriages. An intermarried couple's financial difficulties can involve not having enough money and not agreeing on how to manage their money. The proper management of money is a learned skill that is defined differently by different ethnicities and races.

Theresa, a Caucasian, was very upset by her Chinese husband, Wai-Hong, who sent a monthly check to his widowed mother in Hong Kong. "What bugs me the most is that his mother does not even need the money. Besides, Wai-Hong would not buy me a gift for my birthday, which he considers no big deal," complained Theresa. Again, the manner in which Wai-Hong chose to spend money was culturally determined. Despite the financial status of his mother, Wai-Hong considered it his duty as a son to remember and to honor his mother by sending her money. Furthermore, birthdays (other than one-month, thirtieth, and sixtieth) are not considered eventful among traditional Chinese. While his wife was criticizing his way of spending money, Wai-Hong was puzzled by her lack of respect for him as an honorable son and a thoughtful thrifty husband.

Different Religions

Studies indicate that religious differences can be detrimental to successful marriages (Friedman, 1980). Couples of different races or ethnicities usually share different religions. Different religions teachings and practices often cause misunderstandings and disagreements between an interfaith couple. It is one thing to recognize the fact that differences do exist. It is quite another thing to live with these differences, day in and day out as intermarrieds must do. Problems often persist even when a couple believes they have resolved their differences, because the roots of religion are planted deep.

Some intermarried couples, in order to make their marriages work, reject their religions. Sometimes this is too big a price for an individual or a couple to pay. Without faith, an individual is weakened in his or her internal strength, spirit, and commitment essential to becoming a happy individual and to achieving a successful intermarriage. Divorce statistics consistently reveal that divorced couples show more religious indifference than married couples (Heer, 1980). Marital therapists agree that religious couples tend to work harder to solve their marital problems than nonreligious couples (Ho, 1984).

Sexual Adjustment

Historically, most racial and ethnic groups have ascribed separate and defined roles to males and females. Although these expectations may be quite common, cultural groups differ tremendously in the degree of differentiation of sex roles and in the characteristics of the role. There are also vast differences as to how power is distributed and exercised among males and females. Since cultural orientation has a strong impact on an individual's life, it should come as no surprise that it also affects an individual's sexual relationship with a marital partner. Most discussion of sex in intermarriage center on the issue of birth control, especially when one marital partner is Roman Catholic. However, the role of sex in intermarriage is far broader than that of reproduction and contraception. The sex act is a form of marital behavior by which and through which the married couple develop, express, and enrich their spiritual, physical, and emotional relationship with each other. An individual's attitude towards sex and its role in marriage is derived primarily from religious and cultural beliefs. Throughout history, religious and cultural codes have regulated in considerable detail the conditions under which intercourse may occur, the times on the religious or cultural calendar when it is discouraged or forbidden, position to be assumed, and various other aspects.

Ferando, a Latino, was distressed by his Caucasian wife, Vickie, who hardly responded to him sexually, especially in public. Ferando complained to his wife, "You complain that I am not affectionate toward you, but you always turn me down when I want to make love to you." Vickie explained, "I want you to make love to me with words as well as actions. I can't respond affectionately when I don't feel good toward you and toward our relationship." The couple's sexual problem was related to their communication problem. Despite Ferando's display of physical closeness, he was unaccustomed to expressing deep personal feelings verbally, as Vickie desired. In this instance, Vickie's and Ferando's individual cultures determined the manner in which they expressed their affection, and their differences in expression interfered with their sexual adjustment.

Childrearing Practices

Studies indicate that childrearing practices vary greatly among different racial and ethnic groups. Beyond the practice of childrearing are basic ideas and philosophies, such as the emphasis on independence and individuality, or the value of conformity and obligation. Immigration, acculturation, urbanization, and indualization have disrupted and altered traditions, including childrearing traditions.

The arrival of a child reactivates the intermarried couple's memories of their own early childhood and underscores their childrearing beliefs.

Such beliefs can produce new conflict between a husband and wife. The child can become the symptom of this conflict when he or she begins to display uncertainty, anxiety, rebellion, and difficulty in learning or making friends.

In order to avoid conflicts with a spouse, some intermarried couples adopt a "one-partner-taking-over" policy. To maintain the noninterference strategy, the other partner will need to withdraw emotionally and sometimes physically from the family. Thus, an enmeshment between the controlling parent and the child develops, leaving the other parent (who usually is the father) in the periphery. The controlling parent may be burdened with overresponsibility, and the child may resent this parent.

As an alternative to one spouse being in charge, some intermarried couples raise children by a compartmentalized arrangement—both parents have rigid roles and activities relating to the children. Such an arrangement, unfortunately, can make the children feel that their parents lack total concern and acceptance of them.

Partly due to the magnitude of their cultural differences or their unwillingness to accept disharmony in their relationship, some intermarried couples raise their children by adopting a total hands-off attitude. Since neither parent wants to impose values in deference to the other, the children are left in a vacuum with no model or guidance.

Problems of identification present yet another major stress on the child from an interethnic, and more so from an interracial family. The interracial person, the child of the intermarriage, is not only the embodiment of the parent's racial differences, but is also an individual who must work through a very personal identity question (Kich, 1982). Skin color alone is loaded with social implications. According to Erick Erikson, unresolved racial conflicts will affect the parent's ability to care for the infant in a nurturant way and leave the child with a deep sense of not belonging and insecurity.

ADVANTAGES AND CONTRIBUTIONS OF INTERMARRIAGE

Intermarriage has been treated in the past as an abnormality, defiance, or disgrace. Those who openly object to intermarriage for ethnic or racial reasons unfairly criticize it as a matrimonial "mismatch" or disaster (Jester, 1982). They feel it holds virtually no potential for growth and is doomed to failure. The truth is intermarriage, like any other marriage, in itself is neither good nor bad, right or wrong, successful or unsuccessful; it all depends on the couple involved and what they make of it. There are indications that intermarriage can offer those involved the following unique advantages and contributions (Falicov, 1982, Ho, 1984).

More Thorough Preparation. Due to society's attitudes, the individual contemplating intermarriage can be expected to encounter considerable unsolicited advice and opposition from close friends and relatives. The individual may resent this, but it will at least make him begin to think more seriously about intermarriage. As couples struggle to convince themselves, as well as others, of the suitability and desirability of their intermarriage, they are likely to take time to consider seriously the future of their relationship. Such projections and serious discussions enable the couple to think, feel, and plan beyond their present romantic feelings. Thus, they deepen their commitment and increase the likelihood of their marriage succeeding.

Greater Degree of Commitment. Commitment in a marriage refers to an agreement or understanding between husband and wife that their marital union is for a lifetime. A committed couple gives top priority to resolving difficulties and problems that come up in their marriage. Couples of the same ethnic or racial background, who have encountered relatively mild or no opposition (perhaps even encouragement) from parents or friends, may not be as committed as an intermarried couple who has had to struggle every step to make their marriage a reality. Since intermarriages often develop in a rather hostile environment, the couple is forced into a more self-reliant position. Upon making the decision to intermarry, the individual realizes that he or she can no longer depend upon sympathetic supporters to make the marriage work. Whether the intermarriage succeeds or not will be contingent mainly upon the couple's determination and willingness to make it work. Such couples, having faced initial opposition, are usually strengthened in their commitment to make their marriage succeed.

Greater Degree of Self-Other Differentiation. Among the many benefits intermarriage provides is the opportunity to understand and to accept oneself. Most individuals take their values and beliefs for granted. The commonalities one shares with friends, family, and spouse provide comfort and complacency. When an individual's partner is of a different race or ethnicity, this difference forces the individual to be more aware of and to work toward gaining recognition and acceptance of his or her own identity. Only through respecting and accepting one's own identity can an individual genuinely respect and accept his or her partner's identity.

Greater Degree of Acceptance, Tolerance, and Respect. A couple's recognition of cultural and ethnic differences is one important step toward building a successful intermarriage. Marriages between individuals of the same race and ethnicity function as one entity, and husband and wife may be reluctant to acknowledge differences. An intermarried couple is highly aware and accepting of their cultural differences. These differences are constantly visible and are usually reinforced by those around them. The couple feels little threat to their sense of individuality when one partner is confronted by the other who thinks, feels, and behaves differently. As the couple accepts each other's differences, they have no need to be critical or feel defensive. Their mutual acceptance frees them to truly be themselves.

Broader Opportunities for Learning and Growth. A couple of different racial and ethnic background has ample opportunity to learn from each other. To mature as an individual, learning is a continuous process; but real learning often occurs if one is allowed and encouraged to be different. Such learning requires a conducive environment and challenging stimuli, which often a partner from a different background provides.

Greater Opportunities and Perspectives for Children. Through exposure to both parent's racial and ethnic cultures, children from a successful intermarriage have a greater opportunity to learn and to express themselves. They are likely to have a heightened awareness, a harmonious integration of themselves and their environment, and satisfying relationships. The opportunity for assimilation and integration of both their parents' backgrounds can make children of intermarriages more "cultured" than children with parents from the same racial or ethnic background (Collins, 1984).

Children More Accepting of Differences in Others. A child's relationship with others depends a great deal upon his or her ability to accept differences in others. If parents with the same racial and ethnic backgrounds do not expose their child to different ways of thinking, he/she may find it difficult to accept differences. The child of an intermarriage, on the other hand, lives and interacts with differences every day. When this child is faced with strange and new ideas or behavior in others, he or she is better equipped to accept and react positively to these differences.

Greater Vitality in Family Living. There is clear evidence that families plagued by problems are families with few activities and limited interactions in the home (Stinnett and DeFrain, 1986). Since family members do not engage in fun and pleasurable activities together, they become more vulnerable to and intolerant of family conflict and crisis. The diversity in an intermarriage often assures that there is not lack of activity in the family. With a variety of interests and pursuits, and observance of different ethnic festivities, life is rarely boring. Opportunities abound for family members to express their affection for each other. Members of intermarried families have a sense of belonging, stability, identity, and continuity that are essential to their social, psychological, emotional, and spiritual development.

The above discussion summarized some of the realities of the racial and ethnic intermarried. The next chapter will explore and specify the role which culture plays in the intermarried couple's interaction especially as it relates to problem-solving.

Chapter 2

CULTURAL PERSPECTIVES ON PROBLEM-SOLVING

Culture, in one of its simplest means, refers to the widely shared customs and traditions of a specific homogeneous population. In such a social entity, marriage is established according to customs which specify eligible partners, ways of negotiating the marriage, and behaviors and relationships appropriate in marriage. Presumably all marriages in a homogeneous social group occur within the same population segment. Realistically, of course, this is not the case, because many individuals choose to marry someone from a culture different from their own. As explained in Chapter 1, intermarriage is currently on the increase.

Intermarriage brings together two people who may differ in race, ethnicity, customs, traditions, behavior, and in how they perceive and solve their personal problems. The intermarried couple will naturally encounter adjustment difficulties because of their many differences (Reiss, 1976).

The following discussion aims to acquaint clinicians with some of the cultural perspectives that can influence how couples define and solve their problems. When professionals understand the different value orientations of each spouse, they will be better equipped to serve intermarried clients effectively. This, in turn, can enhance a couple's chances of maintaining a successful intermarriage.

Conflicting Value Orientations

Differing cultural values are a major problem in intermarriage because each partner tends to feel that his or her particular culturally ordained values are incontestably "right." This quality of essential rightness is inherent in value systems, for each culture tends to teach that its particular value system represents the most appropriate way to conduct one's life. A marital spouse visually does not recognize that he or she subscribes to a particular set of values until challenged by a partner whose value system is different. Once the individual's value system is challenged, especially by a spouse, the individual becomes uncertain and most often reacts defensively. This behavior then increases marital problems.

For the most part, the ethnic differences described in family therapy literature embody common cultural stereotypes. Recent studies on ethnic cultural value differences suggest that certain ethnic-family stereotypes may have some validity (McGolddrick and Rohrbaugh, 1987; Hotstede, 1980). Some of these ethnic cultural value differences are presented here to sensitize clinicians who counsel intermarried couples.

A major dimension of cultural variation is individualism−collectivism. Individualism is characterized by the subordination of a group's goal to a person's own goal. It is a cultural pattern found in most northern and western regions of Europe and in North America. Individualism is assumed to be a relatively stable and important attribute of U.S. samples (Bellah et al., 1985; Inkeles, 1983). American ethnic populations of German, Greek, Irish, Italian, Jewish, Polish, Norwegian, and British origins commonly exhibit the attribute of individualism (McGoldrick et al., 1982). Collectivism is characterized by individuals subordinating their personal goals to the goals of designated collectives. It is a cultural pattern commonly found in Asia, Africa, South America, and the Pacific. American ethnic minorities such as Asians, Blacks, Hispanics, and American Indians share the characteristics of collectivism (Spiegel, 1971).

In both individualist and collectivist cultures, one can find individuals who are allocentric (pay primary attention to the needs of the group) or idiocentric (pay more attention to their own needs than to the needs of others). To assist intermarried couples with problem solving, it is insufficient just to know the ethnic identification and cultures of the couple. It is also necessary to know some demographic and biographic information, because individuals from an urban, industrialized, mobile, migrating, acculturated, affluent environment with much exposure to the mass media, are likely to be idiocentric even if they come from collective cultures.

Table 2.1 summarizes and contrasts values, attitudes, the self, activities, and behaviors between the collectivist and the individualist. These variables are chosen because they have a predictive value in understanding how an individual from a particular culture behaves and interacts with another individual from another culture and ethnic group.

Table 2.1.
**Differences Between Collectivism and Individualism
in Values, Attitudes, the Self, and Activities and Behavior**

	Collectivist (Asian, Black, Hispanic, American Indians)	*Individualist* (German, Greek, Irish, Jewish, Polish, Norwegian, British)
Values	Harmony, Face Saving, Filial piety, Moderation, Thrift, Equality. Fulfillment of other's needs, Social relationship, status determined by age, sex, family name and place of birth.	Freedom, Honesty, Social recognition, Comfort, Hedonism, and Equity. Contractual relationship. Status is determined by personal achievement.
Attitudes	Strong extended family ties, Strong belief in vertical relationship (father-son), Acceptance of difference in power. Belief in intergroup competition, Dislike interpersonal competition, Cooperation encouraged within the ingroup. Poor "joiners" of the new groups. Ingroup confrontation is taboo. Unprepared in negotiation, Common friend accepted as mediator, Prefer long-term relationships.	Weak extended family ties, Belief in horizontal relationship (friend-friend; spouse-spouse), Acceptance of horizontal relationship. Competition is acceptable at all levels. Super "joiners" of new group, Superficial social relationship. Confrontation is acceptable. Well prepared in negotiation. Prefer short-term relationships.
The Self	Self totally absorbed in the collective, Self is defined as part of a group. Attachment to group is strong. One is what one's group does. A change in ingroups can produce major changes in attitudes and behavior.	Self is autonomous and separate from group. Attachment to group is weak. One is what one does.
Activities & Behaviors	Obligation to attend social events, Strong mutual support, Distrust of outgroups, Need the protection of ingroups, Show more subordination to ingroup than to outgroup	Somewhat detached from ingroups, Trust outsider to a greater extent, More relaxed with outgroup members, Strong work attachment.

Table 2.1. (Continued)

	Collectivist (Asian, Black, Hispanic, American Indians)	Individualist (German, Greek, Irish, Jewish, Polish, Norwegian, British)
Activities & Behaviors Continued	authorities, Strong family attachment. Social behavior tends to be long-term, intensive, involuntary, and occurs mostly within a few groups. Frequent consultation with others in vertical relationship. Strong needs for affiliation, nurturance.	Social behavior tends to be short-term, voluntary, less intensive, and involves little commitment. Fewer consultations, strong need for autonomy.

It is important to remember that individualist cultures differ among themselves, and so do collectivist cultures. Moreover, there can be wide individual differences among people within a culture. The summary in Table 2.1 is intended as general information, not as hard-and-fast rules for dealing with a specific person from a specific culture. Moreover, the factors that contribute to success or failure in a marriage are extremely complex and cannot be reduced merely to cultural commonalities and differences. Because of the enormous complexity and variety of racial and ethnic marriages, it is extremely difficult to make generalizations that are useful to clinicians without delving further into the attendant family processes. The following section discusses different family structures and their relationships.

Different Family Structures

One prime factor influencing an intermarried couple's response to stress and problem-solving is the organizational structure of each partner's own family prior to the conflict. In intermarriage, each spouse provides the contact link between the family of origin and the married couple. Each partner represents two family systems and processes input, both conscious and unconscious, about generational patterns and how to form a successful marriage. In looking outward from the family of origin towards a marital partner, each is searching for a complementary other. The system that intermarried partners form can be understood by viewing it through the filter of their original cultural and familial contexts. Often intermarried couples are not aware that they are caught up in a powerful, mutually reciprocal set of projection processes, with each spouse projecting traits internalized from his or her original family into the intermarital system. To develop a workable partnership, an intermarried couple must understand and respect each other's ethnic backgrounds, values, and behavioral styles.

According to Bowen (1978), anxiety increases in one or both partners when they allow emotional forces to dominate intellectual functioning. If the partners are still intensely emotionally influenced by their families of origin, they may bring unfinished aspects from their family into interactions with each other. When that unfinished business hovers about, meaningful negotiation between marital partners is difficult or impossible. When either partner copes with the original family's emotionality by merging into or totally separating from that family (as many intermarried couples do), problems between the intermarried couple are likely to persist.

Family structure refers to the repetitive patterns of interaction that become routine and, for the most part, operate out of the awareness of family members. Structure is distinguished from process by its resistance to, or slower rate of change rather than by any physical properties (Minuchin, 1974). Research studies indicate that family functioning and wellness are related to family structure (Lewis et al., 1976). In a smoothly functioning family, a high level of both interpersonal closeness and individuality is demonstrated. Communication is clear and spontaneous, and problem-solving is effective, with negotiation a central process. A wide range of affective expressions is apparent, and the parental coalition is strong and characterized by shared power and psychological intimacy. These families are flexible and receptive to a wide variety of family processes under different contextual circumstances.

Dysfunctional families are characterized by rigid, fixed, internal mechanisms that are either dominant-submissive or chronically conflicted, both of which contribute to interpersonal distance. These families are often affectively stifled, and there is underlying anger and sadness.

Current belief in the origin of family organization follows the epigenetic or developmental theory (Wynne, 1984). This theory suggests more or less orderly, developmental phases in the life of the family, with each phase containing certain culturally prescribed tasks or challenges. The ways in which the marital couple begins early in their relationship to grapple with and to resolve these tasks provide the basic building blocks of what will become the family's organizational structure. The ease or difficulty with which the marital couple deals with these tasks again depends heavily on the similarities and differences in each partner's cultural and ethnic upbringing *and* their ability to transform these differences.

To produce an optimal family structure, three developmental challenges need to be overcome. These challenges are commitment, power, and closeness (Lewis, 1976). The process of commitment involves a shift of each spouse's primary commitment away from his or her family of origin to their own marital relationship. Power involves a couple's agreement as to "Who decides what?" and "How are conflicts resolved?" Closeness refers to the couple's established balance of separateness and attachment.

Table 2.2 summarizes different family structures of various ethnic and racial groups. The structural relationships included, kinship ties, husband/wife, parent/child, and siblings, are those that form the basis for understanding and negotiating behavior of the intermarried couple.

Ethnic minority extended family ties are more cohesive and extensive than kinship relationships among the white population (Padilla, Carlos, and Keefe, 1976; Stack, 1974; Martin and Martin, 1978; Skimkin et al., 1978). The extended family of all ethnic minority groups includes life-long friends also. The extended family network represents a relational field characterized by intense personal exchanges that have unending effects upon one's perception, value system, and behavior. The influence of culture and ethnicity on mate selection and husband/wife relationships is very powerful and will be discussed in the next section of this chapter.

The parental functions of both Asians and Hispanics follow the cultural prescriptions for the husband-wife relationship. The father disciplines and controls, while the mother provides nurturance and support. Within an American Indian family, the basic parental disciplining role may be shared among relatives of several generations. The American Indian parent-child relationship is less pressured and more equalitarian than that of other ethnic groups. They respect each child's unique individuality. A black mother is generally recognized for her devotion to and care of her children, while a black father's involvement with his children may be hindered by economic restrictions. Parents of Asian, Hispanic, and black children usually engender the respect of their children through complementary transactions. They maintain parent-child relationships and do not seek to be friends with their children.

Table 2.2.
Ethnic Minority and White American Family Structures: A Comparative Summary

Ethnic Families	Family Structural Relationships			
	Kinship Tie	Husband/Wife	Parent/Child	Siblings
Minority Families				
Asian Americans	Extended family	Patriarchal	Hierarchical	Hierarchical by age & sex
American Indians	Extended family	Patriarchal/ Matriarchal	Eqalitarian	Eqalitarian
Black Americans	Extended family	Eqalitarian	Hierarchical	Hierarchical
Hispanic Americans	Extended family	Patriarchal	Hierarchical	Hierarchical by age & sex
White American Families				
German	Nuclear	Patriarchal	Hierarchical	Hierarchical by age & sex
Greek	Extended family	Patriarchal	Hierarchical	Hierarchical by age & sex
Irish	Extended family	Matriarchal	Hierarchical	Eqalitarian
Italian	Extended family	Patriarchal	Hierarchical	Hierarchical by age & sex
Jewish	Extended family	Patriarchal	Hierarchical	Hierarchical by age & sex
Polish	Extended family	Patriarchal/ Eqalitarian	Hierarchical	Eqalitarian
Norwegian	Extended family	Patriarchal	Hierarchical	Eqalitarian
British	Nuclear	Eqalitarian	Hierarchical/ Eqalitarian	Hierarchical by age

The sibling relationship is influenced by Asian's and Hispanic's vertical hierarchical structure and male dominance. There is no distinct favoritism afforded to the American Indian or black child. Older siblings of all minority groups are accorded authority to supervise and take care of younger siblings, and this minimizes sibling rivalry.

Of all the white American ethnic groups, British and German groups stand out as less reliant on extended family relationships. British families partially make up the group of Americans known as WASPS: White Anglo Saxon Protestants, the epitome of American culture. This ethnic group has been in the United States longer than the others, colonizing this country in the early 1600s. British Americans are taught that individual effort overcomes almost any external restraints. The family is experienced and valued as it sustains the individual, not the other way around. It was largely the British American family which created the 20th century ideal of a nuclear family.

Parent/child interaction of all white ethnic families generally adheres to a hierarchical structure. In Greek families, children are included in most activities and are rarely left with babysitters. Parental feelings are usually not articulated and children are given advice and direction instead. In Italian families, the father is the head of the household and the mother is the heart. Jewish Americans encourage verbal interaction and children's opinions are highly valued. The concept of Mitzvah, or obligation, is central in Jewish tradition, creating many expectations between parents and children.

Children are raised in Polish families with strict discipline and respect for their parents. The father has chief responsibility for this. Children get the message that they are being disciplined for what they have done and not because they are bad children. This is quite different from the Irish Catholic message of personal badness. Norwegian children are supposed to learn what is expected without much discipline. Each child is seen to have a unique inborn potential and individuality, but is cautioned against expressing it openly.

Sibling relationships among certain white American groups are influenced by vertical hierarchical structure and male role dominance, as seen in German, Greek, Italian, and Jewish cultures. There is no clear favoritism afforded to the Irish, Polish, and Norwegian child. An older British child, regardless of gender role, may be afforded authority to supervise younger siblings.

When an individual intermarries, he is faced with integrating his own family structure with that of his partner. The couple's success or failure in doing this again depends partly on the similarities and differences of the two families of origin. The following discussion will present and contrast husband-wife interactions within different ethnic groups. How the husband and wife interact in their intermarriage is greatly influenced by how their own parents interacted. The husband brings to the new marriage his set of experiences and memories of how his father and mother related to each other, and the same is true for his wife. To a large degree we learn how to behave in our own marriage by having observed, while growing up in our parents' home, how our parents behaved and interacted as a couple.

Mate Selection and Husband-Wife Relationship

Among the ethnic minority groups, there is considerable similarity between Asian Americans, American Indians, and Hispanic Americans. The tradition of arranged marriage is gradually disappearing because of migration and acculturation. The choice of mate, however, is still heavily influenced by the families of both sides. Extended family ties also exert a strong influence, and elders of these ethnic groups encourage their young people to marry within their own group (Hippler, 1974; Stevens, 1973; Brown and Shaughnessy, 1982). It is difficult for courtship even to begin if the families disapprove.

The patriarchal system of Asian Americans, some American Indians, and Hispanic Americans place the wife in a low status position in the family structure. Traditionally, Eskimo men treated their wives as inferior and were reluctant to have close interpersonal contact (Hippler, 1974). American Indian women, independent for the most part, played a submissive role to their husbands (Hanson, 1980). The Hispanic wife is expected to care for the home and to keep the family together; her husband is not expected to assume household tasks or help with the children. Such traditional arrangements sometimes result in wives assuming power behind the scenes, while overtly supporting their husband's authority (Brown and Shaughnessy, 1982).

The husband-wife relationship of a black couple has been more eqalitarian than the above three ethnic minority groups, and even more so than for most white groups. This is partly a result of their African heritage, in which the culture did not "denigrate the independence of women nor define a man by the dependency of his woman" (Mullings, 1985, p. 18), and partly a consequence of slavery, which required women to work. Women of all ethnic minority groups consider motherhood a more important role than that of a wife (Hsu, 1972; Stevens, 1973; Bell,

1971). Given that it is the existence of children that validates and cements the marriage, motherly love is a much greater force than wifely love.

Minority women, intermarried or not, must cope with contradictions resulting from their ethnicity and gender status. If a minority woman intermarries with a man from a different minority group, these demands can multiply and exacerbate her functioning as an individual and as a marital partner. Within the marriage, a minority woman is expected to remain strong, loving, tender, and nurturing, and to hold the family together, even if there are meager resources. She is expected to support, sustain, and nurture a mate who is likely to be unemployed or under-employed. If her husband is adequately employed, she must also support, sustain, and nurture him so that he can cope when faced with threats to his self-esteem. She is expected to teach children, who may grow up in a hostile environment, to be loving and trusting, cautious and strong. Often she is without supportive networks. A minority wife and mother is expected to feel valued, although given low status and low-paying jobs (Rodgers-Rose, 1980). She holds the nuclear family together and copes with stress attendant to the loss of the extended family. Finally, she is expected to cope with three value systems: that of her minority group, her husband's minority system, and larger dominant group or population.

Irish is the only ethnicity among White Americans in which the wife occupies a dominant role in the marriage. Irish women are seen as strong, independent, dominant, and morally superior to men. Irish culture is matriarchal with fathers often shadowy or absent figures. Respect, not love, is the binding tie with Poles, and the husband is the head of the household. The wife maintains control of the requisite dowry after marriage. Present-day Polish American women usually contribute significantly to the family income.

British Americans generally view marriage as a contractual relationship for the purpose of individual needs, sex, money, and the pursuit of happiness. Marital communication is often dominated by conversations about business.

In German families, the husband is the dominant partner in the marriage. He is generally reserved and strict. The German wife often is emotionally more powerful in the family, although for outside appearances, she never challenges her husband's leadership. The marital bond and division of labor in German households solidifies the roles of a rational, dominant leader, who is the husband, and an emotional, submissive nurturer who is the wife.

Italian husbands like to be viewed as the head of the household. The status of Italian wives is somewhat paradoxical. They are considered servers of men and yet play powerful roles, especially in their sons' affections. Mutual support and complementary roles have been more important for this group than marital sharing of emotions or intimacy.

A Jewish man is commonly perceived as a good husband, father, and provider, and a Jewish woman is often seen as a devoted wife and mother of intelligent children. Some Jewish men may suffer the paradox of achieving position and prestige outside the home while feeling unappreciated or ignored within the family. Jewish women also experience conflicts over home obligations and careers. Family, academic achievement, and financial success are generally important to both the husband and the wife.

Norwegian families are patriarchal; however, women are expected to work and earn money. Emotional expression between a husband and wife is strictly controlled. Aggression is channeled indirectly by teasing, ignoring, or silence.

Help-Seeking Patterns

There has been no study that explores the help-seeking patterns of intermarrieds. However, there is ample evidence which indicates sharp differences between middle-class white Americans and ethnic minority clients in the way they seek help for family and marital conflicts. Ethnic minority clients do not consider psychotherapy a solution to their emotional and marital problems (Kleinman and Lin, 1981; Casas and Keefe, 1978; De Geyndt, 1973; McAdoo, 1977). Minority clients' underutilization of counseling and psychological services can be attributed to a variety of reasons: (1) distrust of therapists, especially white therapists; (2) cultural and social class differences between therapists and clients; (3) lack of bicultural and bilingual therapists; (4) overuse or misuse of medical staff for psychological and interpersonal problems; (5) language barriers; (6) reluctance to recognize their need for help; (7) lack of awareness of the existence of counseling services.

It is generally agreed that the socialization of Blacks in America has conditioned them to reveal themselves reluctantly to white therapists (Vontress, 1976). On the other hand, Blacks have been found to risk openness more willingly with black as opposed to white therapists (Wetzel and Wright, 1983). Racially similar therapist-client dyads have resulted in greater self-exploration (Banks, 1972).

The clear-cut demarcations between the sexes in some traditional ethnic cultures may affect therapist-client relations and outcome. Paddilla (1981) found, for example, that some Hispanic male clients have trouble discussing their sexual concerns with female therapists. Conversely, most Hispanic women prefer to discuss their personal problems with a female (Hynes and Werbin, 1977).

All ethnic minorities consider the family and extended family their primary source of support. When natural support systems are unavailable, most ethnic minority clients or families consult their folk healers or religious leaders. When all these fail, the family *may* consider seeking help from the mainstream family and health care system.

Help-seeking patterns of intermarried couples closely correspond to their specific needs and to their cultural backgrounds. Intermarried couples who are newly arrived immigrants seek information, referrals, advocacy, and English-language instruction, but seldom want therapy. Intermarried couples who are highly acculturated and speak English well may seek marital therapy. Knowing the help-seeking patterns among various ethnic groups gives the therapist general information about what to expect from an intermarried couple. This is particularly useful during the initial stage of therapy. A brief orientation of marital therapy by the therapist may be helpful, especially to non-Whites or new immigrants (Acosta, 1977). The next chapter will examine the theoretical perspective for intermarriage therapy.

As the above discussion has indicated, there are many variables to consider when helping intermarried couples with problem resolution. Of prime importance is a therapist's sensitivity to cultural differences between the couple in seeking help, defining and analyzing problems, and in resolving differences.

Chapter 3

THEORETICAL BASIS FOR INTERMARRIAGE THERAPY

Marital therapy has become a major mode of therapeutic intervention in the last decade, because it can help alleviate marital distress and facilitate adult intimacy and family cohesion. Many disorders, such as depression and agoraphobia, previously treated as intrapsychic issues are now treated in a marital context (Rounsaville & Chevron, 1982). Marital therapy also has been regarded as having the most potential to create change across the family level of functioning (Lewis et al., 1976).

The wide acceptance of the marital therapy approach to problem solving has generated many treatment theories and models. Unfortunately, the philosophical orientations and the techniques employed by some of those theoretical approaches may diametrically oppose the indigenous cultural values and family structures of the intermarried who share two different cultures. It is clear that marital therapy with intermarried couples requires an organized, culturally sensitive theoretical framework. Such a conceptual framework should take into account the intermarried couple's reality, culture, biculturalism, ethnicity status, language, social class, original family structure and help-seeking patterns.

This chapter will discuss the ecosystemic approach and the family life-cycle framework. Marital and family therapy theories and their application are also detailed. The chapter concludes with an examination of the transcultural framework that is important in all phases of therapy with intermarried couples.

The Ecosystemic Approach

Many theories of family and marital therapy are directed at the process of conflict, anxiety, and defense systems within the individual or the family (Feldman, 1986; Stuart, 1980; Ackerman, 1961). The ecosystem approach maintains that imbalance and conflict may arise from any focus in the transactional field. Uric Brontenbreuner originally developed an ecological model in 1977 utilizing four factors affecting human development and interaction: individual, family, culture, and environment. An ecosystems model is presented in Figure 3-1.

Although the couple or interpersonal relationship is the primary

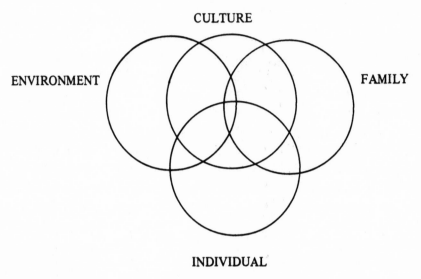

Figure 3.1. Ecosystems model for analysis of psychosocial factors impacting on intermarried couples

concern of marital therapy, problem-solving and enhancement of the marital relationship cannot occur without clear analysis of the four ecological factors. The level of emphasis upon each of these factors, in turn, depends on the specific nature of the couple's problem. At the individual level, the focus is on the biopsychological endowment each person possesses, including their personality strengths, level of psychosocial development, cognition, perception, problem-solving skills, emotional temperament, habit formation, and communication and language skills.

The family level focuses on family life style, culture, family organization, sex role structure, division of labor, affective style, tradition, rituals, life cycle expectations and adjustment, and management of internal or external stress. The nature and quality of the spousal relationship and the depth of connectedness to children and extended family also are areas of concern in the analysis and enhancement of a couple relationship.

At the culture level, the focus should be on understanding the value systems, belief systems, the societal norms of the host culture, and, in the case of ethnic minorities, the original culture. Cultural conflicts can also result in marital conflicts and mental-emotional impairment.

At the environment level, the focus should be on understanding the economic and social structure of American society which oppresses individuals in the minority groups. Negative societal stereotypes, discrimination, and nonacceptance of the intermarried are other important factors that can affect an intermarried couple's relationship.

An ecological perspective allows a marital therapist to focus on adaptive (and maladaptive) transactions between the couple and between the couple and their environment, that is, the interface between them. There are several therapeutic principles that are particularly relevant to therapy that uses the ecosystem framework with the intermarried. Four of these therapeutic principles are discussed below.

First, individual or couple relationship problems are seldom conceived as an illness. Problems or difficulties are understood as a lack or deficit in the environment (as in the case of newly immigrated military wives), as dysfunctional transactions between systems (social services organization and mental health care delivery systems), as adaptive strategies (cultural shock and conflict). A therapist can focus on the interface between or among systems or subsystems.

Second, the principle of equifinality allows and encourages the therapist to apply a number of different interventions which produce similar effects or outcomes. Such flexibility and creativity in seeking alternative routes to change provide the therapist the option to relate interventive strategies to existing couple therapy theories, or to apply innovative strategies of change based on the client's unique cultural background and life space.

Third, therapeutic strategies make use of the life experiences and natural systems of the client or couple. Emphasis on the client's life space and family as a natural helping system places the therapist in a role as cultural broker instead of intruder or manipulator.

Finally, the ecological principle that a change in one part of the system impacts on all other parts of the system allows the therapist the flexibility to intervene within a marital situation without involving both spouses in the change process. Thus working with one marital partner may well bring about significant change in the couple relationship when couple interactions are rigidified by traditional role structure, or when one spouse is not amenable to couple therapy, the one-to-one therapeutic modality may be the only workable resolution.

The ecosystemic framework is particularly helpful to a therapist in organizing and evaluating data during the assessment phase of therapy. Other systemic marital and family therapy theories also are organized and presented here according to their specific usefulness in relation to the intermarried couple's developmental needs and presenting problems.

Family Life-Cycle Framework

Transitions through the expected developmental phases of the family (Glick and Kessler, 1980; Carter and McGoldrick, 1980) have major implications for racial and ethnic themes. An individual's need for a positive sense of cultural identity and continuity with past traditions, far from diminishing, increases over the life cycle (Gelfand and Kutzik, 1979). Couples involved in intermarriage sometimes deny their different-ness and abandon their cultural rituals. This usually causes a loss of family connectedness and changes the continuity of the family life cycle. A spouse who leaves his or her country of origin to marry may later experience a painful longing for homeland and roots. Sometimes the total impact of a decision to intermarry may be experienced only after complex new family structures are in place or when a full resolution of loyalty conflicts cannot be achieved.

Many intermarried couples may not experience problems in their relationship until later in life. The birth of a child precipitates wishes to share happiness, concerns, and anxieties with one's own parents. It is also a time when families rally together to support the new couple. The birth of a child to the intermarried couple may symbolize the transforma-tion of two cultures into a new system. Parents of the intermarried who have been resistant to the marriage up to this point often shift their relationship toward the couple.

The transformation of two cultures after the birth of a child is a complicated task. Not knowing how to integrate their cultural patterns, the couple may decide to raise the child by creating a new culture and ignoring the past. This sometimes upsets grandparents who do not want their grandchildren raised with different beliefs and values. Sometimes new parents may resent grandparents and cut them and their past off.

When the system remains closed to the past, couples tend to become isolated and child-focused, increasing the probability that the children will become symptomatic.

When children reach latency and adolescence, they can relate to grandparents directly. This necessitates renegotiation of family patterns and relationship across three generations. The need for cultural continuity also increases when children leave home or when family members are ill or die. The couple's adaptation to a new family pattern can impact on their marital relationship. When children leave home, parents often feel a need for closer connections to their own parents. A new desire for closer connections with one's own cultural roots can cause difficulties in a normal marital relationship.

Retirement, reduced activity, approaching death, or the death of a spouse can reawaken needs for cultural ties. This need to reclaim one's cultural identity at certain moments in the life cycle is difficult to anticipate and may create stress on the marriage.

In attempting to understand intermarriage conflicts, it is important to assess how the couple interacts with life-cycle stresses. Intermarriage requires a degree of flexibility and adaptation not necessary for those who marry within their own group. There will always be certain differences in values, emotional reactions, and world views which an intermarried couple may never be able to integrate or harmonize. A therapist's awareness of this fact is crucial in helping the couple to resolve cultural and marital problems.

Applying Marital and Family Therapy Theories

Within the ecological systemic framework, marital and family therapy theories fall into two major categories: structural and communicative-interactive theories (Levande, 1976). Marital and family therapy theories can be logically and systematically applied to work with the intermarried by adopting William Schutz's Fundamental Interpersonal Relations Orientation (FIRO) framework (Schutz, 1958). A few family researchers (Robbins and Tooney, 1976; Wynne, 1984; Lewis, 1976; and Doherty and Colangelo, 1984) also have used this model in couple relationship building, marriage enrichment programs, and family treatment. The FIRO model can be quite relevant and useful in organizing marital and family therapy theories to work with the intermarried.

Inclusion. The interpersonal need for inclusion is defined as the "need to maintain a satisfactory relationship with respect to interaction and association" (Schutz, 1958, p. 19). Inclusion issues in a marriage are those which center around membership and boundaries (i.e., the extent to which the marital couple is part of the society/community and the extent to which each marital spouse is part of, but at the same time apart from, the family or extended family units). Lewis (1976), in his study of strong marital systems, refers to the inclusion process as commitment which involves a shift of each spouse's primary commitment away from his or her family of origin to their own marital relationship. Major factors which may contribute directly or indirectly to an intermarried couple's disharmony and lack of inclusion are (1) economic survival, (2) society's disapproving attitudes and practices, (3) loss of extended family and support systems of one or both spouses, and (4) cultural conflicts, especially those centering around sex roles and childrearing practices.

Control. Schutz (1958) defines control as the need to establish and maintain a satisfactory relationship with people with respect to influence and power. Power involves a couple's agreement as to "Who decides what?" and "How are conflicts resolved?" Satisfactory control relations include a balance between controlling and being controlled in relation to others, as well as the ability to offer and receive respect. The issues of control and power are basic to the intermarried couple's ability to solve problems. How these issues are handled requires a clear understanding of cultural upbringing on the part of each spouse.

Affection. Schutz (1958) defines affection as the need to "establish and maintain a satisfactory relation with others with respect to love and affection" (p. 20). Satisfactory affection includes a balance of initiating and receiving close, personal interactions. Schutz further stresses that "affection is a dyadic relation: it can occur only between pairs of people at any one time."

Hence, inclusion in the FIRO model concerns primarily, but not exclusively, the *formation* of the relation, while control and affection center on relations *already formed.* Schutz concludes, "Generally speaking, inclusion is concerned with the problem of in or out, control with top or bottom, and affection with close or far" (1958, p. 24).

By extending Schutz's FIRO model and theory of group (couple) development, the inclusion issue has to be dealt with first, the control issue second, and affection or the intimacy issue last. This order of treatment has great significance and application in working with the intermarrieds. Most intermarried couples, especially those where one partner is from an ethnic minority group, do not rely on social or psychological theories to account for behavioral or marital difficulties (Lapug, 1973). Recently arrived immigrant or migrated intermarried couples direct most of their energy simply to adjusting to a completely new environment. In addition, intermarried couples who experience vast cultural conflicts with each other, with the extended families, and with the host community or country may also struggle with the inclusion issue. Hence, the inclusion issue that involves membership or couple-community interface and couple extended family system boundaries generally is the area the couple is willing to work on. Only after the inclusion issue has been successfully dealt with can the control and intimacy issues be openly discussed with the couple. It is also important to stress that while all three FIRO issues are always present in couples, the emphasis changes according to the couple's degree of acculturation, the couple's family life-cycle stage, individual partner personality, dynamic, and other life circumstances.

In analyzing the specific emphasis of major contemporary schools or marital and family therapy, one finds that all of them tend to focus on one of the Family FIRO issues of inclusion, control, or intimacy. Table 3.1 links the major schools of marital and family therapy with the FIRO issues with which they are most closely identified.

The relevance of structure marital therapy with the intermarried lies with its emphasis on the couple as a boundary-maintaining social system in constant transition with its immediate environment or other political/social systems. Hence, marital therapy as guided by this conceptualization suggests two levels of intervention: strengthening the boundary-

Table 3.1
Categorization of Marital and Therapy Theories by FIRO Issues

	Structural	Communication	
Theories Employed	Eco-Structure (Germain/Aponte) Marital, Family Structure (Minuchin/Bowen)	Strategic (Haley/Madanes White)	Humanistic (Satir/Whitaker Greenberg and Johnson)
FIRO Issues	Inclusion	Control	Affection/Intimacy
Therapeutic Emphasis	Marital involvement, membership, boundaries	Power, expectations, rules, decision-making	Bonding, loyalty, friendship

maintaining ability of the couple system for adaptive purposes, or intervention at the broader societal level to reduce destructive environmental influences upon the couple system (Minuchin, 1974; Aponte, 1979).

The communicative framework developed and advanced by Haley (1976) and Madanes (1984) was based on symbolic interaction which places major emphasis on the interactive processes taking place among individual family members and subsystems within the family. Interactive processes that are particularly important in therapy with intermarrieds include power or control issues in communication, conflict resolution, and decision making. Behavioral approaches (Jacobson and Margolin, 1979; Stuart, 1980) to marital therapy also emphasize control issues in marriage by stressing ways in which couples try to influence one another's behavior by overt or covert means.

Whitaker's symbolic experiential (Whitaker and Keith, 1981), Satir's humanistic approach (Satir, 1972), and Greenberg and Johnson's emotionally focused marital therapy (Greenberg and Johnson, 1986) emphasize emotional bonding and intimacy in a marriage. Such issues relate to indepth sharing of thoughts, feelings, and desires that are considered private and a vulnerable part of the self. From the perspective of the bonding theory, marital conflict arises as a result of an insecure bond, involving perceived inaccessibility or emotional unresponsiveness of at least one of the partners. Marital therapy should address each partner's sense of security or conversely, sense of deprivation and isolation in the relationship. It should focus on addressing emotional expressive issues instead of solving instrumental problems.

When a couple presents many issues from the FIRO categories, the therapist should make the theoretically prior category the first goal (i.e., inclusion before control and control before intimacy). In actual practice, the therapist may intervene in such a way that other FIRO issues are addressed simultaneously; however, the primary goal should address the theoretically prior category. The next section will discuss how the therapist can use a transcultural framework in actual therapy with the intermarrieds.

Transcultural Framework

The therapeutic advantages of therapist-client ethnocultural similarity are inconclusive (Cortese, 1979; Jones, 1978). However, research does demonstrate that a therapist's effectiveness tends to depend on his or her perceived credibility (Sue, 1981). Griffith (1977) further elaborates that despite the therapeutic orientation, one of the crucial factors in successful therapy seems to be the therapist's understanding and sensitivity to the marital couple's ethnocultural background. It is essential to understand the biculturalism of clients in a cross-cultural setting in order to work effectively with biracial and bicultural couples.

In transcultural couple therapy, the goal is to help the couple clarify their personal and cultural standards and expectations within the marriage. In order to accomplish this, the transcultural therapist needs to understand the couple's respective racial or ethnic group and the dominant group culture and know the points of contact between the two cultures. The therapist should also know how the cultural standards of each influence each spouse and the marital relationship itself.

The transcultural therapist should identify with the help of the couple what *aspect* of couple conflict is attributable to the sociopolitical environment, family structure, marital structural, and individual dynamics. Regardless of the ecosystemic structure the therapist chooses to focus on, the prevailing influence of racial and ethnic factors of each partner involved must be considered.

By considering the couple's cultural background, the therapist can better understand the couple's life strategy, the physical, conceptual, emotional, behavioral, metaphysical components. A transcultural therapist is obligated to understand a client and his or her transaction in a marital relationship within the *client's* cultural context, to refrain from generalizing beyond what is known, and to retain an attitude of hypothesis and skepticism with regard to one's own understanding of other people. Additionally, a therapist will use his or her knowledge of a culture and a tentative hypothesis about cultural patterns of thinking, feeling, and acting as a basis for recognition of those patterns and their meanings if and when they are presented by the client. This is never imposed on the client or the couple, nor is one aspect of behavior linked beyond its presentation to a general culture or ethnic pattern, unless more of the pattern emerges. The use of cultural knowledge parallels that of developmental psychology and systems functioning, and it prohibits the use of ethnic or racial labels in treatment.

By employing the transcultural framework in couple therapy, cultural knowledge can be applied differentially and strategically during various treatment phases.

The Engagement Phase

Forming a therapeutic relationship with an intermarried couple has aspects of cultural joining and becomes a "cultural relationship." The engagement phase focuses on validating and affirming, at least via recognition, the family, the cultural roots, and the intermarriage. It is important to identify the couple's individual cultural style of forming trusting relationships, especially help-seeking relationships. While an American Jewish man may have little hesitancy in seeking professional marital therapy, his Asian wife may be reluctant to disclose her private life to a stranger totally unrelated to the family. The therapist may need to reassure and validate the Asian wife's willingness to seek professional help as a sign of an honorable reflection of her commitment and loyalty to a family relationship. The therapist needs to know also what the couple expects from the therapist. A therapist's ability "to leave" temporarily her own culture and to analyze the couple's relationship is critical during this engagement stage of therapy. A therapist's willingness to try to use the couple's manners and language can convey understanding and trust. Couple therapy with one therapist may risk a triangulation process with the therapist siding with one spouse. This risk increases if the therapist's racial and ethnic background is the same as one spouse. The therapist's own gender also may affirm one spouse and at the same time alienate the other spouse. At the engagement stage of marital therapy, the therapist should try to join the couple as a unit instead of joining one spouse only.

Marital Problem Identification Phase

Much of what distinguishes one culture from another and distinguishes subcultures within a large pluralistic society is shown in the diverse ways in which people perceive and report their experiences, including the experiences of stress stemming from marital crises. Language is of particular importance, since it is the symbolic device by which the flow of that experience is categorized, labeled, evaluated, and acted upon. Language is a key to the components of any presenting problem and the best way to find out what the couple thinks is stressful and dysfunctional is to ask: "What is your idea (thinking, understanding, etc.) of what is not working? How did it come about? What have you tried to do about it? What do you think needs to be done now?"

In therapy with an intermarried couple it is important to recognize that the couple's experience of a problem or crisis is both a personal and a social event. It is personal in that it disrupts the daily routines of individuals by creating discomfort and pain. It is social and cultural in that the labeling of experience often requires confirmation from others before corrective action can be taken. Hence, the therapist's acknowledgement of the role of socially significant others in the couple's life is critical in the identification and evaluation of personal or marital problems.

The Intervention Phase

The intervention stage is characterized by the therapist successfully moving toward the intermarried couple culturally. The therapist demonstrates flexibility and gives the couple opportunities to respond to their problems in a new manner. Change in couple therapy sometimes indicates a change of modification in the couple's cultural strategy. This may involve learning to restore, expand, or modify the cultural stress response pattern.

The therapist needs to suggest changes by using traditional, culturally acceptable language. Instead of discarding the couple's old pattern of coping, the therapist may suggest that the couple "keep doing what they have been doing." This becomes the foundation for adding something new or trying something different. As much as possible, the new strategy or suggested change must be presented as an extension of the "old" cultural stress response. For example, as a British American husband is supported by the therapist to be self-contained in response to stress created by a rebelling teenage son, his Hispanic wife's over involvement with her son also is validated by the therapist. The therapist's alternate encouragement of the husband to help his wife be calm and of the wife to show her husband how to be emotionally involved with their son helped the couple restore their spousal subsystem. If the British American husband's self-sufficiency and his Hispanic wife's child-centered life strategies were not validated and supported, the couple's defense would be further rigidified and new change or strategy toward couple relationship enhancement might not materialize.

The Ending Phase

The end phase of intermarried therapy should reconnect and restore the couple to their large world or environment. This is accomplished through incorporating the new changes in the couple's original life strategy independent of the therapist's interaction. For example, after therapy, the British American husband needs to feel adequately self-contained even though he has integrated much more interpersonal emotional expressiveness toward his son and wife. Similarily, the Hispanic wife needs to feel that being a good mother is important although she has learned that being emotionally close to her husband not only enhances her marital relationship, but also her relationship with her son.

The ending phase of transcultural intermarried therapy affirms there are new paths to old goals. Cultural affirmation and expansion are effective and ethical ways to improve a couple's adaptation and functioning.

Part I of this book has discussed the reality of intermarriage, the cultural perspectives on problem-solving, and the theoretical basis for intermarriage therapy. Part II will be devoted to the actual application of methods, techniques, and skills in intermarriage therapy.

PART II
TECHNIQUES AND SKILLS IN
INTERMARRIAGE THERAPY

Therapy with interracial or interethnic couples presents special needs and considerations, regardless of the race or ethnic background of the therapist. If they are not adequately aware of or sensitive to the complex dynamics of the multiracial or multiethnic system, therapists may unknowingly drive away their clients after the initial session. An *over emphasis* on race or ethnicity as major determinants of the couple's problem can also be ineffective to therapy. Stereotypes, beliefs, and values about ethnicity, race, and intermarriage are important considerations in the assessment and treatment process, but an effective therapist must also maintain an appropriate balance. Chapter 4 will focus on the engagement and assessment processes of intermarried therapy. Chapter 5 will be devoted to the application of ethnic-competent skills and techniques in therapy with the intermarried.

Chapter 4

ENGAGEMENT AND ASSESSMENT STAGE

ENGAGING THE INTERMARRIED COUPLE

The engagement phase of therapy with intermarried couples is a critical period. This phase of therapy is very important due to several factors. In an attempt to minimize their differences, intermarried couples have a tendency to de-emphasize the reality and the urgency of their conflicts. They often have no knowledge of what marital therapy is about. If the intermarried couple involves a spouse from a collectivist culture, especially Asian or Hispanic, that partner may feel uncomfortable seeing a marital therapist. Relying on a marital therapist, who is an outsider, to resolve private marital problems can create feelings of betrayal of one's parents and extended families. For an American Indian or black spouse, marital therapy may be an unwelcome intrusion to self-determination and individuality. Most racial and ethnic minority clients are uncomfortable with "talk" therapy and are self-conscious of their English language deficiency.

Partly due to limited financial resources, intermarried couples are seldom self-referred for continuous therapy help. Many intermarried couples have contact with therapists only because they are referred by mainstream societal agencies such as schools, mental and health care agencies, the court, or social service agencies. If this engagement phase of therapy is not "properly" conducted, the first interview will most likely be the last time the therapist will have contact with the couple.

In intermarriage therapy, the racial or ethnic backgrounds of the therapist and of the couple become important, because they are immediately visible and can be quickly identified and utilized by any of the participants. A strong positive or negative identification might cause the therapist to lose objectivity, and, therefore, render a disservice to the couple. The ethnic or racial background of the therapist can also be an excuse for one spouse not to continue or cooperate with therapy. Therefore, at the beginning of therapy, the ethnic and racial background of the therapist should be brought into the open and clarified (Ho and McDowell, 1973). The therapist may choose to express his or her desire to remain neutral and his or her wish that both partners feel free to speak up if they think the therapist is not being neutral. Should the couple express discomfort about the therapist's ethnic or racial background, the therapist may involve a cotherapist of a different background. This will help assure that the therapist does not, even subconsciously, take sides with one spouse at the expense of the other.

The sex and age of the therapist is another factor that can cause some intermarried couples to underutilize marital therapy. Some men, especially American Asians and Hispanics, may feel awkward and embarrassed to discuss their private, intimate problems with a young female therapist. They respect the therapist to be authoritative and wise, and in many cultures, a young woman is not viewed this way.

Because of a long history of discrimination, some ethnic minority Americans find it difficult to trust a therapist who represents the majority system. It is important that as early as possible the therapist define his or her role with the couple. There is a need to orient intermarried couples in how to use marital therapy. This may involve exploring with the couple their expectations of the therapy, the role of the therapist, and their degree of involvement during the therapeutic process.

Because the therapist is often perceived as an authority figure, she or he needs to assume an active role during the engagement phase of therapy. To minimize the unnaturalness of the initial therapist-couple contact, Minuchin's maintenance technique, which "requires the therapist to be organized by the basic rules that regulate the transactional process" in a specific couple system (1974, p. 175), is helpful. For example, if the couple consists of a Hispanic husband and an Asian wife, given that the social interaction of the Hispanic American is governed by a hierarchical role structure, the therapist should address the husband first. If one spouse is an American Indian, the therapist should allow ample time for the couple to gather their thoughts and emotions before pressing on to a new topic. Most frequently, the intermarried couple is overwhelmed by multiple problems, and they will feel considerable anxiety about seeking help. It is not advisable to inform the couple at this engagement stage that therapy may be long-term and difficult.

Use of Bilingualism and Interpreters

In intermarriage therapy, one frequently meets couples who speak bidialectal or nonstandard English (SE). In some instances, one spouse may be bilingual and the other may speak no English at all. The therapist's use of SE with a bidialectal or non-English (NE) speaking client or couple can itself affect the therapeutic relationship. Intermarried clients sometimes become conditioned to react to all SE speakers in a similar manner and to expect similar behavior from them. The couple, in fact, may stereotype SE speakers, including the therapist, and act in a socially distant or subservient manner. This presents problems in intermarriage therapy where an intimate working (nonauthoritarian) relationship is sought.

A therapist needs to be sensitive to behavior cues that language-based stereotypes evoke. These cues may include a client or couple continually addressing the therapist by his or her surname and title while presenting themselves in a subservient and dependent manner. Another cue is when the client insists on concrete answers and quick solutions, the therapist should realize that the client is simply behaving in the therapeutic situation, in the same manner he does with all formal interactions. The possibility always exists that the client's use of a nonstandard English can lead to a misdiagnosis and a distorted conceptualization of the marital situation. When presented with a client or couple who speaks nonstandard English, the therapist should automatically assume that his or her judgment and objectivity are going to be compromised. The only questions that remain are how much and in what manner.

To maximize the benefit of intermarriage therapy, the therapist needs to encourage the client or couple to speak in the manner that he or she speaks to natural confidants. Explore with the couple who they share intimate information with. Encourage them to become comfortable using the speech style they traditionally use when sharing intimate information. If possible, the therapist can encourage this by using part of, or completely switching to, the client's preferred dialect (Rozensky and Gomez, 1983). If the therapist is incapable of doing this, he can at least show acceptance of the couple's use of nonstandard forms. One of the best ways for the therapist to communicate respect for NE is to plead ignorance and encourage the client to "teach" him or her the language. The therapist can also show acceptance of NE forms by acknowledging that some forms of nonstandard language exist in every speech. The therapist should be careful not to appear disrespectful or condescending when dealing with language differences.

To maximize the subtleties and nuances in therapy with NE-speaking clients or couples, the therapist may need to use reflective paraphrasing more liberally than usual. The following excerpt from a marital therapy session between a NE-speaking client (Korean wife) and a SE-speaking therapist demonstrates how paraphrasing and questioning can be used to prevent potential misunderstandings.

Client: It be's that way . . . you know . . . don't nobody care nothin' about you except if they somethin' in it for them.

Therapist: I hear you say nobody cares about you as a person?

Client: Yeah, I guess you could say it like that.

Therapist: I like for you to help me explain "it be's that way."

Client: Well, I mean that way—it be's that way . . . ain't nobody cared about me, not my father or mother who are still in Korea, my husband . . . what's use.

Therapist: So you mean nobody cares, nobody's there that you can count on, not even your husband. You don't see much hope for it to be different.

Client: Yeah.

To show respect for clients it is important that the therapist use part of the client's own language and paraphrase in such a manner that he does not appear to be correcting the client.

If the therapist ascertains that the therapy assessment is being hampered by one spouse's use of non-SE, he should enlist the help of a consultant who has a wider range of experience or who can speak the spouse's dialect. The following case illustrates the appropriate use of a consultant, as well as the way in which language affects the dynamics of an intermarried family therapy session:

A Hispanic consultant was called in on a case in which a White female therapist was seeing a biracial (Hispanic mother and white father) adolescent in family therapy. The therapist had made a good connection with the adolescent and his father, but the mother seemed uninvolved in the sessions. The therapist's initial impression of the family's dynamics was that the mother maintained a disengaged and emotionally detached role in the family. The therapist, however, was not confident with her initial formulation for she realized that the mother did show considerable involvement with her son outside the therapeutic setting.

The consultant pointed out that the mother was much less fluent in SE than the father or the adolescent, and that since the sessions were conducted in SE, the mother was clearly at a disadvantage. The consultant saw the family jointly with the therapist for several sessions, and through the case of Hispanic NE phrases interspersed within SE, the mother began talking and taking a much more active role in the therapy sessions. Later, the therapist was able to interact alone with the family by asking the father to act as interpreter from Hispanic NE to SE.

It should be pointed out that the use of one spouse as an interpreter can have negative effects in intermarried couple therapy. The spouse who is the interpreter can be perceived as more powerful than the other spouse. Triangulation between spouse, interpreter, and the therapist can diminish the therapy process and outcome. The spouse-interpreter can also use the interpretation to his or her advantage at the expense of the couple's relationship.

Considering the large number of non-English speaking people in the United States, it is essential that intermarried couple therapy at times be conducted with the aid of an outside interpreter. For such therapy to take place effectively, the interpreter must be carefully selected and oriented (Glasser, 1983). Ideally, the culture of the interpreter and the couple or the non-English speaking spouse should be the same. Any prejudices the interpreter or the non-English speaking spouse has related to the social, economic, and class status or sex of the other can interfere with the therapeutic process and outcome. The interpreter must understand his or her role in the therapeutic process. That role is to serve as a conduit linking the therapist with the couple. Ideally, the interpreter is a neutral party who neither adds nor subtracts from what the primary parties communicate. It is the duty of the interpreter to inform the therapist or the couple when a question or comment is unclear or unacceptable. The interpreter communicates not only with words but also with gestures, emotional expressions, and varying intonations. He or she must have the capacity to act exactly as the therapist acts and express the same feelings.

When an interpreter is used, the couple should be assured of confidentiality early in the first interview to encourage them to express themselves and to discuss sensitive issues. The therapist should explain the interpreter's presence and role and assure the couple of the interpreter's neutrality and confidentiality.

Transitional Mapping and Data Collection

Pertinent personal, familial, and community information and cultural mapping are extremely helpful in the assessment of an intermarried couple, particularly those who undergo social change and cultural transitions, such as new immigrants. The therapist should establish which phase of the process of immigration the individual or couple is currently in and how they have dealt (as a couple or individually) with the vicissitudes of previous phases (Sluzk, 1979, p. 389). Additionally, cultural specific factors relevant to each partner's life experiences must be ascertained. Examples include: Personal data, such as language and dialect spoken, physical health and medical history, work roles, and help-seeking behavior patterns. Other significant demographic information is also important, including how many years the couple has lived in the United States, country of origin, immigration status, and so on.

Psychological data that are helpful in the assessment phase of interracial or interethnic couple therapy include the spouse's process of adaptation and acculturation, and past problem-solving ability. The degree of life cycle interruption can be significant, especially if the couple's marriage was not supported by the extended families. Other social and cultural data such as the spouse(s) immigration and relocation history, work environment, and extent of contact with other support systems (such as churches, friends, and human service networks), will help the therapist to assess the couple's degree of support or stress from the external environment.

A sociocultural map should also include the transitional position of the multigenerational families of the couple. The technique of cultural mapping is very similar to the technique of constructing a genogram (Pendagast and Sherman, 1977). In taking a genogram, a therapist inquires systematically into family patterns among aunts, uncles, siblings, grandparents, and so on, in an attempt to gather information about patterns of closeness, distance, and conflict. While a genogram generally assists in understanding multigenerational patterns and influences, that is, the history of the presenting couple's difficulties, it also provides the therapist and the couple some insights into how the couple wishes the problem to be resolved (Nachtel, 1982).

In constructing a genogram with an intermarried couple, the therapist needs to phrase highly structured questions, such as, "Who did your mother go to when she got mad at your father?" or "How did your parents exchange affection or resolve conflicts," carefully and, if possible, spontaneously. The couple should be encouraged to share background information with pride and not simply as a means to disentangle present couple problems.

Mutual Goal Setting

The problem inherent in the process of mutual goal setting with an intermarried couple stems from their different perceptions of the marriage and different perceptions of the therapist. The therapist's knowledge and receptivity toward the couple's respective cultures is crucial, not only in the problem identification process, but also later in the therapy stage.

Generally, the therapist who is professionally trained in an individualist cultural orientation will have less difficulty in identifying with the partner who is from the same cultural group. Particularly during the formulation of marital treatment goals, it is the partner from the collectivist culture, of which the therapist generally is unfamiliar, who complicates the process of mutual goal formulation. Due to cultural dissimilarity, this same partner may perceive the therapist as siding with the spouse. Therefore, as a rule, the therapist needs to make a special effort to be culturally neutral and to remain in a position of cultural objectivity when assisting the couple in formulating goals. The goals must be consistent with the couple's "transitional culture," not just the husband's or the wife's own culture.

As one spouse individually expresses concerns and desires for the marriage, the therapist's role is to elicit feedback from the other spouse. Goal formulation with intermarried couples can be time consuming and extraordinarily complicated. The therapist needs time to comprehend the couple's cultural and linguistic differences. Often an individual partner needs confirmation and validation of his or her struggle and efforts already invested in the marriage, regardless of how dysfunctional or inappropriate those efforts may have been.

Many problems experienced by intermarried couples, especially those who are newly arrived immigrants or from the lower socioeconomic class, are social and involve learning to cope with environmental stresses. The therapist's responsiveness to the couple's request for immediate, concrete services is important. The therapist can also act occasionally as the couple's advocate. The therapist's willingness to help can lead to the couple trusting the therapist enough to express other more intimate marital problems.

Therapeutic goals with intermarried couples can be divided into five categories: (1) therapeutic goals related to situational stress, (2) therapeutic goals related to cultural conflicts in cultural code and transition, (3) therapeutic goals related to cultural stereotyping, maximizing and minimizing of cultural differences, (4) therapeutic goals related to the family-life cycle and extended family ties, and (5) therapeutic goals related to idiosyncratic problems in marriage.

Situational stress occurs at the interface between the couple and the new environment. Problems may include social isolation, cultural adjustment, unfamiliarity with community resources, or poverty. An intermarried couple of different nationalities or who is new to this country often experiences situational stress. Dysfunctional patterns of cultural transition are interactional patterns that were once adaptive to one's cultural environment and context but later became rigid in the couple's interaction and adaptation. An example of a cultural conflict in cultural code is the patriarchal German husband who refuses to allow his matriarchal Irish wife to enter into an egalitarian relationship. Such couple conflicts may also manifest themselves in financial management, child-rearing practices, communication, and intimacy. Some intermarried couples use their cultural differences stereotypically against each other to create a makeshift boundary that prevents painful emotional involvement during times of great stress. In problems related to family life cycles, the couple's conflicts are often tied to the realignment of boundaries with the extended families who may disapprove and not support the intermarriage.

Some intermarried couples have difficulties in being either too close or too separate. Clinically such couples find themselves unable to live together or to part from one another. The marital bonds are in a continual state of disequilibrium. Previous or current perceptions of their experiences in intimate relationships with significant others often contribute to the problem. Couple idiosyncratic difficulties may also include personality developmental impasses which affect personal functioning and interpersonal relationships. Some problems appear at different times in a couple's life span. Others may be more salient throughout the marriage. For example, at the beginning of a couple's marriage, the couple focuses on the development of a common cultural code for defense against the families of origin. Hidden cultural differences begin to surface as the couple moves from the couple life stage to the parent-child life stage. Children force the couple to interface with the families of origin. Failure to adapt to the interface and other life events may provoke rigid, negative stereotyping by each partner. That reinforces idiosyncratic problems interfering with couple bonding and intimacy.

The process of mutual goal formulation requires that the therapist be cognizant of the conflicting value orientations many intermarried couples face. For instance, many minority clients are brought up with interdependent or collectivist values that conflict sharply with the independent or individualist values held by the spouse from the dominant cultures and usually including the therapist (Acosta et al. 1982). A spouse from a collectivist group is not likely to formulate therapy goals that will benefit himself or herself only. Similarly, the significance attached to the parent-child, especially mother-child, dyad is much more important than the marital dyad in a collectivist culture. Although the child's presenting problem may be attributed to a dysfunctional marital relationship, therapy goals focusing on repairing the marital subsystem at the onset of therapy will be strongly resisted. Conversely, therapy goals focusing on the parent-child relationship challenge the collectivist-orientation and also possibly the wife's desire to be a good mother. By learning how to perform dutifully in a mother-child relationship, the mother may be willing to learn how to interact differently with her husband.

Intermarried couples involving a minority spouse, especially new immigrants, find it difficult to admit they have emotional or psychological difficulties. Acknowledging such problems arouses considerable shame and a source of having failed one's family. Minority clients will respond more favorably if they perceive the treatment goals as an obligatory means to meet such concrete needs as employment, shelter, and a warm and harmonious home environment for their children. The couple's acceptance of such a treatment goal is consistent with their traditional social explanation of disorienting events. This type explanation of a treatment goal also allows the individual to see himself or herself as a victim of some unfortunate but uncontrollable event, a result of non-personal determinants.

Most intermarried couples find loosely targeted and abstract long-term goals incomprehensible, unreachable, and impractical. They prefer structured and goal-directed work with clear, realistic, concrete, and measurable objectives. A therapist should not rule out the possibility, however, that some interethnic or interracial couples, who are highly acculturated and fluent in English, may respond well to highly insightful therapy related to intimacy issues. Couples receiving this type of therapy should be carefully screened, and such therapy should not be attempted without a strong therapist-couple relationship.

SELECTING A FOCUS/SYSTEM UNIT FOR THERAPY

Generally, selecting a focus or system unit for intermarriage therapy depends largely on how the problem is defined and what the treatment goals are. However, due to the multifaceted nature of intermarriage, selecting a system unit for therapy requires special consideration. A husband and wife who have different cultural backgrounds may define the same problem differently. They may differ as to how the problem should be solved. The therapist needs to know which therapeutic modalities can best facilitate areas of conflict in the couple relationship. The therapist should be culturally aware and sensitive to how each spouse in the intermarriage responds to different therapeutic treatment modalities.

Use of an Eco-Map

According to the ecosystemic framework, conflicts within an intermarriage emanate from a variety of ecological factors. An eco-map is helpful in selecting a focus for intermarriage therapy. The eco-map, as developed by Hartman (1979), is a paper and pencil simulation that portrays in a dynamic way the ecological system whose boundaries include the client or couple in the life space. It identifies and characterizes the significant supportive or conflict-laden connections between the intermarried couple and their environment. It makes available a more comprehensive picture of the major themes and patterns that can direct the goal formulation and therapeutic target and keep both therapist and couple from getting lost in detail.

Specifically, the eco-map provides three major criteria to help the couple and the therapist select a plan or unit of intervention. These criteria are outlined below.

(1) The couple in relation to their ecological environment. Evaluate the kinds of significant material, physical, spiritual, social, or health care resources that are available or unavailable in the couple's world and

information pertaining to the couple and environment relationship (strong, stressed, and so forth). Some interracial and interethnic couples experience political, social, and psychological isolation. Intervention directed toward the interface between the couple and the environment may be the most crucial and therapeutic for such couples, rather than focusing on couple interaction and intimacy issues.

(2) The couple-environment boundary as measured by the number and quality of transactions. To protect against discriminatory practices from society, former friends and extended family members who disapprove of their intermarriage, some intermarried couples isolate themselves from the external environment. Such couples may be closed off from new sources of energy and in danger of moving toward a state of entropy, that is, of enmeshment, disorganization, and ultimately dissolution.

(3) The relationship within the family and its connection with the outside world. When the husband is employed outside the home, it will affect his role and relationship with his wife. When the wife first works outside the home, or becomes overly active in church activities, it will affect her relationship with her husband.

A therapist working with an intermarried couple will find the eco-map practical and easy to use (see Figure 7.1). The three criteria outlined provide a sound base from which to work with the couple to select an appropriate focus/system unit for therapy. Let us now look at some possible choices.

Conjoint Couple Therapy

Intermarried couple therapy is most beneficial when the therapist sees the couple together, that is, in conjoint couple therapy. The couple's interaction in therapy will often give a clearer picture of what contributes to their presenting problem(s). By observing the couple's interactive style, conceptualization and resolution of problems, verbal and nonverbal communication, and problem-solving skills, the therapist can use conjoint therapy as a means and a context for problem-solving. In addition to gaining a broader and more complete understanding of their problems through couple immediate feedback and interaction, conjoint therapy provides the couple with a live and natural environment under the direction and guidance of the therapist. The couple can learn alternative and effective ways of communicating and problem-solving with each other. The couple's learning that occurs in conjoint therapy is not limited to intellectual understanding. They also learn how to make effective and behavioral changes as well.

One-to-One Therapy

As beneficial and desirable as conjoint therapy may appear, there are times often in the beginning stage of the therapy when this modality is not appropriate. The therapist should first assess the willingness and readiness of the couple to communicate in a conjoint or group setting. The hierarchical and vertical structure of some collectivist cultures, such as Asian and Hispanic, discourage the wife sharing her true thoughts and negative feelings toward her husband, especially in front of a therapist. There will sometimes be unusual circumstances, such as spouse abuse, child abuse or adultery, etc., where conjoint therapy with the couple at the onset of the therapeutic stage might limit one spouse's participation. Other times one spouse may feel tremendous hurt and pain and need time alone with the therapist to vent his or her feelings in a safer environment without the presence of a threatening spouse. Conjoint therapy under such circumstances will be contraindicated at this early stage of therapy and if pursued will only intensify the couple's negative feelings and interaction with each other. Using conjoint therapy in adverse situations can also cause the therapist at times to misdiagnose the couple's problem and resources for therapy.

One-to-one therapy is indicated when one or both partners feels the need to be listened to nonjudgmentally and unconditionally. It provides the therapist with an opportunity to establish trust and rapport with the couple individually. When the individual spouse realizes the therapist is empathic and can be trusted, he or she will tend to disclose intimate or toxic information essential to the accurate assessment and ultimate resolution of the marital problem.

When interviewing a spouse individually, the therapist needs to guard against conducting individual therapy with the spouse. Although the spouse is seen in a one-to-one context, the objective remains the improvement of the *marital* relationship. Seeing a spouse individually in couple therapy should be defined as transitional and temporary only. As soon as it is feasible, the therapist should suggest to the couple that conjoint therapy is in order.

Family Therapy

A couple's relationship is sometimes affected by other members of the family. Different child-rearing practices between the intermarried is a common problem. To alleviate couple conflicts, at times it is essential to interview the whole family, including the children, as a unit. It is important for the therapist to understand that in collectivist cultures, such as Asian, Hispanic, and some American Indian tribes, family members are not encouraged to share their true thoughts and negative feelings together. For parents to express fear or sadness openly in front of children indicates in these collectivist cultures that parents are losing control and "losing face," thus abdicating their authoritarian roles. Open expression of negative feelings by children might be interpreted as lack of respect and deference to parents. Such behavior might inflict shame on parents and guilt on the children.

Extended Family Therapy

Extended families impact tremendously on the intermarried, especially when the intermarried involves a spouse from a collectivist culture. If the marriage does not have the support and approval of the extended families, the intermarried couple faces more problems. Often the use of extended family therapy is necessary. Generally, there are two ways extended families can be involved in intermarried couple therapy. The first is to involve the extended families in conjoint family therapy. The objective here is to assess the extent of the extended family's help or hinderance to the intermarried couple's relationship. When necessary the therapist can teach extended family members how to interact differently to help the intermarried couple improve their relationship.

Involving the extended family in conjoint intermarried couple therapy can be very challenging. If the extended family still harbors strong negative feelings toward the intermarried couple, it is best not to involve them. Most extended families like to see their children enjoy a happy marriage, but they are reluctant to realize or to admit the role they play in their children's conflictual marital relationship. At times the extended family wants to help their children but is unwilling to meet conjointly with them. The second way the therapist can involve the extended family is by interviewing the extended families privately. The therapist should give extended family members the opportunity to vent their anger and disappointment over the couple's intermarriage. By interpreting and validating their behavior as the extended family's way of coping with the marriage and even with helping their children, the therapist may be able to win the family's confidence. The therapist will then be in a better position to suggest ways that the family can assist the couple. Hopefully the extended family's relationship with the intermarried couple will improve in the process.

To conclude, a therapist's selection of a focus or system unit for therapy must be based on the nature of the couple's problem(s), data derived from cultural mapping, and, perhaps more importantly, the ability, willingness, and readiness of the couple and other family subsystems to engage in problem solving in a group or conjoint context.

The above discussion deals primarily with the engagement and assessment stage of intermarried couple therapy. The next chapter will be devoted to applications of techniques and skills in therapy with the intermarried.

Chapter 5

PROBLEM-SOLVING STAGE

After a culturally relevant understanding of the intermarried couple's problem has been mutually formulated, the process of implementing a culturally sensitive intervention is in order. The line between understanding the couple's problem and responding to it for the purpose of problem solving is characteristically a fine one. Generally, the intermarried couple will not only have definite ideas of what is conflictual in their relationship, but will also have established patterns of stress responses that reflect their particular culture's life-adaptive strategies.

By the time the problem-solving stage of therapy has been reached, the therapist has already demonstrated the capacity to be culturally adaptive and to relate in a variety of ways. This ensures that the intermarried couple is afforded the opportunity to respond to their conflictual or problematic experiences in new ways. Changes that take place in intermarried couple therapy are, in part, a shift or modification of the cultural life strategy of both spouses. This process requires that the couple learn to restore, expand, or modify the traditional cultural stress response or problem-solving repertoire.

The therapist introduces the change/modification process for the couple by framing the change within traditional framework or language. Basically, the couple is validated in their problem-solving effort. This will form a foundation for adding something new or trying something different in the name of assisting the couple to adjust to their "marital culture" that is in transition. The therapist's new suggestion(s) should be presented as an extension of the couple's "old" cultural stress response. The importance of affirming the foundation of what the couple already has as the necessary precondition for assimilating and then accommodating a new response constitutes a key principle in therapy with an intermarried couple during the problem-solving stage.

There are sixteen generic techniques and skills that are particularly relevant in the problem-solving phase of therapy with intermarried couples. These techniques and skills can be categorized according to the specific therapeutic goals to be accomplished. As stated in Chapter 4, there are five major therapeutic goals characteristic of therapy with the intermarried. These goals involve resolution of (1) situational stress, (2) cultural conflicts in cultural code and transition, (3) cultural stereotyping: minimizing and maximizing of cultural differences, (4) family life-cycle crisis and extended family ties, and (5) idiosyncratic problems in intermarriage. Table 5.1 summarizes goal-related techniques and skills in the problem-solving phase of therapy with the intermarried.

Table 5.1.
Goal-Related Techniques and Skills for the Problem-Solving Phase
of Therapy with Intermarried Couples

Therapeutic Goals				
Situational Stress	*Cultural Conflicts*	*Cultural Stereotyping, Minimizing, Maximizing*	*Family Life-Cycle Crisis*	*Idiosyncratic Problems*
Mobilizing and restructuring the extended family network	Accepting personal differences	Self-observation Paradoxical intervention	Therapy with the extended family	Diagnosing the idiosyncratic problem
Employing role models, mediator role, educator role, and advocate role	Emphasizing World culture Strategic use of cultural issues	Employing the cotherapist approach	Promoting interde-pendence family obligation	Specifying therapeutic goals Working through personality and marital integration
	Social and moral reframing Restructuring cultural taboos		Employing a therapist-helper	

TECHNIQUES AND SKILLS IN
RESOLVING SITUATIONAL STRESS

Situational stress occurs during the interface between the couple and their new environment. Situational problems may include social isolation, discrimination, cultural strangeness, unfamiliarity with community resources, or poverty. Two techniques and skills are relevant in assisting the intermarried in resolving situational stress: (1) mobilizing and restructuring the extended family network, and (2) using role models, such as mediator, educator, or advocate.

Mobilizing and Restructuring the Extended Family Network

The intermarried couple paradigm is defined as a couple's construction of reality (Reiss, 1981). If one or both spouses is from a collectivist culture, the couple will probably have a strong, close-knit extended family and support system. Unfortunately, this system can be severely affected by migration, discrimination, and sometimes isolation if the extended family disapproves of the intermarriage and withdraws their support. Without a strong support system, the intermarried couple may be forced to interact to the extent they become "fused." As a result of fusion, spouses demand too much from each other and, at times, fail to meet their own individual needs and fail to resolve couple conflicts. This is particularly characteristic of an intermarriage where one or both spouses are newly arrived immigrants. As soon as possible, the therapist should assist the couple, or the newly arrived spouse, in establishing a social support network, whereby the couple or the individual spouse can reestablish a greater sense of "differentiation of self" (Bowen, 1978) but at the same time fulfill the couple paradigm needed for social belonging. A social support network can also provide the couple or individual spouse a place to (1) bridge the ecological deficit, (2) form friendships, (3) ventilate frustrations, (4) learn acculturated social skills, and (5) relax and have fun. Upon realizing one's situation is not unique, an individual can view his or her couple problems from a more optimistic and objective perspective.

When the therapist tries to link the couple with an existing social network, the concept of "balance" is vital. Factors essential for balance include matching with existing resources the couple's interracial or interethnic marriage, the couple's and spouses' age, origin of birth, length of stay in this country, socioeconomic class, formal education, language, and religion. In some instances, especially when there is a scarcity of intermarried couples in the community, the therapist may need to identify, recruit, and organize such a social support network. The following case example illustrates the therapist's use of a social network to assist an intermarried couple.

The Baker's family consists of Mr. Baker, a Caucasian, Mrs. Baker, an

American Indian, and Mary, Mrs. Baker's eight-year-old daughter from a former marriage. The Bakers married nine months ago in another state, and they moved into this neighborhood just over three months ago.

The couple was referred for therapy when their marital conflict caused their daughter to miss quite a lot of school. When contacted about their daughter's absences, Mr. and Mrs. Baker displayed no surprise and cooperated with the school official in getting Mary back in school regularly. The couple expressed no interest in couple therapy, and the therapist respected the couple's wish. He volunteered to transport their daughter to school since he happened to live in the same neighborhood as the family. The family accepted the therapist's offer and over the next two weeks, Mrs. Baker did call for the therapist to provide transportation for their daughter. To express the family's gratitude, Mrs. Baker gave the therapist homegrown vegetables. Through this informal exchange, the therapist learned that the family was totally shut off from the community, which Mrs. Baker labeled as "cold" and "unfriendly." After learning that the Bakers were religious individuals who had not been attending church regularly, the therapist referred the couple to an American Indian minister. Mr. Baker first showed signs of reluctance but agreed later to go to church. The minister introduced the Bakers to other interracial couples who attended the same church. Through this extended interaction with other Indians and interracial couples, the Bakers became more relaxed and paid more attention to Mary. Mary began attending school regularly without the therapist's assistance. The Bakers also realized that they still had considerable problems communicating with each other, but they decided to work it out themselves. "Talking it (communication problem) out with other interracial couples just like us helps," declared Mrs. Baker.

Employing Role Models

When an intermarried couple is forced to cope with migration, acculturation, or adaptation to life-cycle changes, it often creates confusion and disorganization for an individual spouse and for the couple relationship. The intermarrieds may already be experiencing loss due to transcultural migration and emotional separation from the family of origin. The feeling of loss and separation is usually more acute for a couple (or a single spouse) from a collectivist culture. At the same time the couple will be concerned with "unattainment" or unfulfillment of basic needs (Pollak, 1964). This type situation can threaten the basic survival of the marriage. In these circumstances, a therapist can most often help the couple by acting as a role model. The role needed may be that of a mediator, educator, or advocate.

Mediator. When the therapist's role is that of a cultural translator or mediator (Auda, 1984; Minuchin, 1974), he should help the couple form an open system with available community resources as quickly as possible. An intermarried couple's dysfunctional patterns often relate directly to the lack of proper role modeling. Traditional role-modeling might have been functional in the past or with a partner of the same race or ethnicity, but it becomes dysfunctional when the couple experiences different cultural norms and life cycles. Hence, the therapist may first need to assume a translator/mediator role and assess which parts of the couple system need translating or mediating.

Being sensitive to the couple's cultures does *not* preclude the therapist's attempting to produce change in areas that restrict the couple's ability to function in their present environment or solve their problems. A therapist's task is not to change the cultural patterns of couple interaction, but to alter those specific patterns that are dysfunctional within the couple relationship. For example, a British-American husband who desires closer interaction with his Jewish American wife will need to learn an eqalitarian model of male-female relationship. Clearly, the power of alignment that characterized the couple relationship will be challenged by presenting a model of transaction in which the husband pays attention to what the wife has to say, in which there is give and take, and in which each partner has a voice in decision making. Particularly helpful according to Satir (1967) and Miller, Nunnally, and Wackman (1975) are family communication skills that include mutual reinforcement, methods of constructive disagreement, the use of feedback, brainstorming, decision-making options, and so on.

Educator Role. When a therapist assumes an educator role, she needs to be sensitive to the intermarried couple's general response that places them in a learner role. Learning in therapy should be problem-focused, short-term, concrete, and specific. This is especially true when there are language difficulties and when one or both spouses are from a culture that is "present oriented." The therapist can educate the couple by immediately identifying inappropriate exchanges as they occur. For instance, if one spouse accuses the other of "never" caring, the therapist can stop the conversation and point out to the accusing spouse the other partner's recent considerate acts. When a spouse fails to display appropriate or caring behavior, the therapist should call attention to it when it occurs. For example, if one spouse expresses loneliness at being neglected at home, but displays no discernable emotion, the therapist can explain that the individual's unusual outward calmness and reserve probably did not reflect his or her inner feelings of fear or sadness.

There are times when a couple fails to identify or express their feelings and it impedes the problem-solving process. The therapist may use her own feelings to make a point as a way to educate to the couple appropriate behavior for meaningful exchanges. For example, if one spouse is calmly reflecting the injustice he or she received from inlaws or others who discriminate, the therapist can comment, "That angers me!" Teaching the couple to interact by modeling, the therapist demonstrates that it is possible to be loving without being controlling, and critical without being punitive.

Teaching a couple how to express intimate feelings is quite different from teaching them where to secure concrete services to meet their basic needs. As a rule, teaching is more effective if the couple *asks* for it and is ready to implement the new information. Normally, a couple will appreciate and make use of new knowledge to secure concrete services. They will be more reluctant to adopt a new interactive pattern that may be foreign to their own cultural pattern. It is important that a therapist not assume an educator role prematurely or prior to developing a trusting relationship with the couple. Any therapist taking an educative approach should be careful to acknowledge the couple's sincere effort to resolve their problems. This will help prevent the couple feeling the therapist is culturally insensitive or disrespectful.

Advocate Role. Many intermarried couples and families, especially those who are in the lower social-economic class or those who do not possess legal immigration documents, are the victims of social injustice. At times, an intermarried couple's space can be invaded with well-intentioned but uncoordinate, inappropriate, and even destructive interventions. For example, an intermarried couple with an immigrant spouse who receives psychological counseling can be inundated with recommendations from a language teacher, a nurse, a social service worker, and a psychologist. The English teacher may say the client's psychological problem is caused by a language barrier; the nurse may advise the client to get more rest. Meanwhile, the social worker may be taking the client for job interviews as a means to meet the couple's basic needs, while the psychologist insists that the client is so disoriented that she needs hospitalization. The client's husband, needless to say, will feel considerable confusion and anxiety.

A therapist can assist an intermarried couple in such a situation by acting as the couple's advocate. The therapist should help the couple prioritize and coordinate all the services they receive so the couple will not be fragmented. Sometimes the therapist may have to assume a biased position in order to get the couple to arrive at a workable solution to its problem. In view of the couple's general feelings of powerlessness, it is important that the therapist's advocating efforts be realistic. The therapist should avoid drawing attention to the couple or subjecting them to further agency humiliation or discrimination.

TECHNIQUES AND SKILLS IN RESOLVING CONFLICTS IN CULTURAL CODE AND TRANSITION

When working with interracial or interethnic couples, it is helpful for the therapist to focus on differences in cultural values pertaining to marriage and family organization. Collectivist cultures emphasize values that maintain contact and continuity between a married couple and the extended family; individualist cultures favor more discontinuity and emotional autonomy from the family of origin. Such differences in rules governing inclusion and exclusion of others in the marriage and in rules about power and authority have a great impact on intermarriages. These rules constitute cultural code that organizes expectations about marriage both internally and in relation to other subsystems (Falicov and Brudner-White, 1983).

Moreover, dysfunctional patterns of cultural transition are interactional patterns that once adapted to one's cultural environment may later become rigid and dysfunctional in the couple's current interaction and adaptation. The techniques and skills useful in resolving cultural conflicts include: accepting personal differences, emphasizing the world culture; strategic use of cultural issues; cultural reframing, and restructuring cultural taboos.

Accepting Personal Differences

During the courtship stage, two people of different race or ethnicity may be very much attracted to each other's differentness. After marriage, the same couple may find that opposites no longer attract and may actually annoy the spouse. For example, in an Irish/Italian marriage, the Italian spouse frequently seems warm, passionate, and sensuous to the Irish spouse, whereas the Irish spouse may seem to the Italian spouse very independent, prudent, and able to handle stress with humor rather than drama. As the marriage matures, the Irish spouse's tendency to resolve a problem by distance may be intolerable for the Italian who interprets distance and separation as disloyalty. Meanwhile the intense emotional display of the Italian spouse may devastate the Irish partner. The couple's behavioral patterns are often interpreted and treated as individual psychopathology problems instead of ethnic attitudes or traits.

To help the couple overcome their cultural conflicts, the therapist can ask the couple to relate prior experiences or couple interactions that endeared them to each other. Questions such as, "What attracted you to each other when you were courting?" or "What made you decide to get married?" may help the couple to recognize that the spouses' behavior has basically remained unchanged, but their *perception* of each other has altered, because each feels attacked instead of admired. An impersonal focus on cultural differences, instead of individual psychopathology, lessens the couple's threat of personal assault. As the couple feels supported and not judged and criticized, they are more likely to refocus their problems by identifying and understanding their respective cultural backgrounds. They can then work jointly to modify their expectations of each other as a means to resolve their conflicts.

Emphasizing the World Culture

In an effort to achieve mutual adaptation, intermarried couples often either minimize or maximize their cultural differences and end up with only a superficial knowledge about the other spouse's culture. This kind of couple interaction prevents negotiation in important areas and impedes the development of a new cultural code or world culture.

Theresa, a Caucasian, was very upset by her Chinese husband, Wai-Hong, for sending a monthly check to his widowed mother in Hong Kong. "What bugs me the most is that his mother does not even need the money. Besides, Wai-Hong would not buy me a gift for my birthday which he considers no big deal," complained Theresa. Again, the manner in which Wai-Hong chose to spend money was culturally determined. Despite the financial status of his mother, Wai-Hong considered it his duty as a son to remember and to honor his mother by sending her money.

Sending his mother money had a great deal to do with Wai-Hong's adherence to the perceived role as his mother's caretaker in a psychological sense, especially after his father died. Wai-Hong's dutiful behavior also was his way of reclaiming his own cultural identity. Being an American naturalized citizen living close to his in-laws, Wai-Hong felt the monthly check to his mother brought him comfort and eased his guilt at not being able to be home taking care of her.

After the cultural dynamic of Wai-Hong's behavior was revealed, Theresa expressed relief that her husband's behavior was not a direct attack on her. She began to disclose some other good qualities of her husband, including his loyalty and genuine love for his mother. Theresa further disclosed that her own family was never close and that she wanted special closeness from her husband. The world view or world culture of family closeness then became the focus of the couple's discussion. Wai-Hong finally admitted that he could be more loving and affectionate to his wife. Previously he was unable to do so because he had spent all his energy defending himself and his cultural practices against his wife's attacks.

By focusing the discussion on world culture, the couple is able to share commonalities of the family bond each needs. The couple began to realize that they have more than one culture to rely on in their interaction with each other and that they are involved in the process of cultural transition. Wai-Hong realized that his bond with his mother was important, but at the same time, that his relationship with his wife also is important. His relationship with both can exist simultaneously and complementarily. The concept of world culture is unique and should be an integral part of an intermarriage. It can certainly be capitalized on in resolving marital conflicts.

Strategic Use of Cultural Issues

In the process of assisting the intermarried couple in clarifying their cultural conflicts, it is important that the therapist pay attention to the content and also to the process of the couple's interaction. For example, by focusing on Wai-Hong's and Theresa's conflictual relationship (content), attributed to the husband's collectivist orientation and the wife's individualist orientation, without simultaneously focusing on the hurt and pain (process) each feels in the situation, little can be accomplished to resolve the existing conflict. Conversely, a therapist's effort to raise the cultural consciousness of the couple may unwittingly make them feel hopeless. A cultural labeling might suggest that a particular behavior is unchangeable because it is rooted in the culture. For example, the therapist could frame, "Wai-Hong just practices what every properly behaved son would do. He can't help being a good Chinese son." This exonerates him from personal motivation and responsibility. It is better if the therapist can help the couple view a cultural trait as a *resource* rather than an inflexible feature that can be used or not, depending on the circumstances. Sending money home to mother is a cultural trait of Wai-Hong. How much money and how frequently it is sent can be negotiable. It is important that in intermarried couple therapy that the marital partners and the therapist refrain from using culture as a "terminal hypothesis," thus suggesting that a behavior is unchangeable.

To avoid this pitfall, therapeutic interventions that underline cultural differences can be balanced by finding common ideologies or complementary cultural traits. For instance, the complementary bridge between Wai-Hong and Theresa is the emotional bond essential to family life. This bond includes the mother-son *and* husband-wife relationships. To facilitate one bond is also a way to strengthen the other bond. To have a harmonious husband-wife relationship is another way to honor an individual's mother and father.

Cultural Reframing

It is imperative that the therapist join the client on the couple's world view and tailor-make therapeutic interventions accordingly. An important aspect of such interventions is the therapist's deliberate use of the "language" of the client or couple in reframing the conflictual situation. As Watzlawick et al. (1974) describe this process:

> ... successful reframing needs to take into account the views, expectations, reasons, premises—in short, the conceptual framework—of those problems to be changed ... Reframing presupposes that the therapist learn the patient's language. (p. 104)

In cultural conflicts, the couple, as well as the therapist, get caught up in ineffective attempts at first-order change. Given their understanding of the nature, cause(s), and context of the problem, the couple and therapist naturally apply the solution they think will work. If one's understanding of the problem changes, the pool of possible solutions will also change. A therapist, in particular, needs to be ready to abandon "obvious" problem solutions when they have proved ineffective. Finding out from the couple what has not worked in the past is crucial to the successful outcome of therapy. Determining what the couple has tried to do about the conflict, as well as what others have suggested, provides valuable guidance to the therapist about what is not likely to work with a particular couple. Moreover, knowing what advice the couple has resisted helps the therapist understand the couple's world view and hopefully design an effective intervention.

Regardless of the nature and intensity of the marital conflict, a spouse from a collectivist culture (especially Asian, Hispanic, and American Indian) will not do or say anything that will cause a personal indignity or deface the family's name and reputation. For a therapist to hold a client directly responsible for a marital conflict could alienate the client and cause him or her to terminate therapy prematurely. Therapists should focus on alleviating a client's anxiety of blame for the problem by capitalizing on the ecosystem and transactional conception of couple problems. With reduced anxiety, the client can devote more energy to obligatory problem-solving within the marriage. During the course of a parent-child conflict, the therapist can reframe the problem "sociably." He can explain to the clients that the immigration, acculturation, or cross cultural integration process is unsettling for all intermarried families. In the case of an unresolved interpersonal relationship manifesting itself in physical illness, the therapist can "morally" reframe the illness to put it beyond everybody's prediction and control.

During the process of cultural reframing, the therapist should be sensitive to complementary roles in an intermarried couple. For example, a Caucasian's accusatory remark to her husband, "You don't care about me," can be reframed (to her Hispanic husband) "Your wife is wondering what she can do to help you be proud of her?" Another example is a Jewish husband's accusatory remark to his black wife, "You never come home," can be reframed (to the wife) as, "Your husband enjoys your company very much. He wants to know what he can do to influence you to want to spend more time with him." A therapist's reframing may not accurately reflect the true meaning of what was said, but the important underlying message cultural reframing can help to convey to the couple is that both respect each other and that harmonious living is the couple's primary concern. The technique of cultural reframing as a second-order change strategy is further illustrated in the spouse abuse extended case in Chapter 7.

Restructuring Cultural Taboos

Each culture has prohibitions prescribing the proper conduct and functioning of its members. When these prohibitions are violated, an individual and the marriage may suffer consequences. The more traditional an individual is, the more closely he or she will adhere to cultural taboos. Obviously, each taboo has served a vital function for a particular culture at a specific time. As times change, however, and as the individual engages in marriage with a partner from another culture, traditional taboos can cause dysfunctional problems.

Phillip Tiger was from an Indian Hopi Tribe. According to this particular tribe's practice, the wife had primary responsibility for childrearing. The husband's responsibility was to raise his sister's children, especially the male children.

Mr. Tiger's wife, Cathy, was Hispanic. According to Cathy, she fell in love with Phillip simply because he was kind and very gentle to children. When the couple was dating, they occasionally baby-sat Mr. Tiger's sister's children.

When the couple had a baby of their own, Cathy was puzzled at the beginning and got angry later at her husband's refusal to care for their new baby girl. With strong urging by his wife, Phillip reluctantly entered into couple therapy. Phillip was a quiet individual and became very anxious when his wife confronted him with his apathy towards their daughter. After some hesitation, Phillip finally explained that his inactive behavior toward his daughter was in accordance with his culture. Cathy's response to her husband's explanation on the one hand was relief for she realized that Phillip's behavior was not a personal rejection of her or of their daughter. On the other hand, Cathy could not understand why her husband refused to change his traditional cultural practices.

A respected Hopi elder was invited to meet with the couple and the therapist. After consulting with the elder, Phillip realized that his previously learned taboo of shared parental responsibility for his child applied only for marriages within the same tribe. Because his wife was from a different tribe, the prohibition did not apply.

Such cases as the above example occur more frequently in intermarried therapy than most therapists realize. If a client mistrusts the western therapist, such cultural taboos may not be brought into the open for fear of ridicule or disapproval. When the cultural taboo issue is raised, it should never be categorically regarded as client resistance, but carefully examined and respected. Often the therapist may need to seek help from tribal leaders or elders.

TECHNIQUES AND SKILLS IN RESOLVING CONFLICTS IN CULTURAL STEREOTYPING: MINIMIZING OR MAXIMIZING OF CULTURAL DIFFERENCES

The protective quality of using cultural stereotypes to explain the inexplainable or the very painful is common in intermarried couple therapy. In couple or familial structural terms, the cultural stereotyping functions as a desperate boundary-making maneuver to prevent the passage of information between spouses. Cultural stereotyping also serves to create distance where there is too much proximity. From an interventive viewpoint, a therapist needs to respect this protective shield and work around the stereotyping until it becomes possible to deal with it or with the thwarted information. Three techniques and skills are presented here to assist couples who experience cultural stereotyping in their relationship. These include self-observation, paradoxical intervention, and employing the cotherapist approach.

Self-Observation

Self-observation, self-recording, and self-monitoring are interchangeable terms that describe a client's oral or written descriptions and records of personal feelings, behaviors, and thoughts. Self-monitoring has been defined as a two-step process: the individual first recognizes the occurrence of the event, then systematically records the observation (Thorensen and Mahoney, 1974). A third step, charting or graphing the information, increases awareness of the phenomenon and facilitates its assessment and change over time.

Asking a couple to record information about themselves increases their activity and sense of control in the assessment and treatment processes, while decreasing the aura of professional authority which many intermarried couples cannot relate to. As the couple and practitioner discuss the information collected by the couple, they act as collaborators in the therapy assessment and planning process. The therapist often assumes a cultural researcher or consulting role. This transfer of responsibility to the couple is an important step toward empowerment (Solomon, 1976). Many intermarried couples experiencing cultural stereotyping and conflicts feel powerless. They are suspicious of the therapist's commitment to help them, and are not dependent on the "experts' " assessment of their situation. Instead, they become experts about themselves—the sources of the data on which the therapeutic plan is based.

The technique of self-observation helps the couple assess their sterotyping or maximizing their cultural differences. The couple's stereotyping functions as a metaphor of their deeper relationship problems. To help them understand this, the therapist may ask the couple to self-monitor under what circumstances each partner stereotypes the other or maximizes their cultural differences to the point that it becomes irreconcilable. As the couple records their behavior, they begin to realize that when they stereotype, they feel hurt, put-down, rejected, or abandoned. Stereotyping is used as a self-defense mechanism from hurting. Unfortunately, it frequently is interpreted by the spouse as an attack. At this point, the therapeutic process can move away from the stereotyping to areas of real concern to both spouses.

Self-observation can also be used to alter one spouse's perception and behavior of his/her mate.

In an attempt to persuade her German husband to take a more active part in disciplining their teenage son, Mrs. B, a Jewish wife, accused (stereotyped) Mr. B of being "cold" and not wanting to "get off his high chair." When Mr. B finally tried to explain how his effort was constantly undermined by his wife, Mrs. B repeatedly interrupted her husband before he could finish what he had to say. The therapist's attempts to block Mrs. B's interruptions were unsuccessful. The therapist then explained he would sit next to Mr. B and dramatize how Mr. B might feel when he was interrupted. The couple agreed to this plan. As Mr. B continued to explain to his wife how much he resented her stereotyping him as cold and unfeeling and treating him like one of the kids, Mrs. B got angry and said, "As far as I'm concerned, the way you have been acting, you are worse than my kids." The therapist immediately dropped down on the floor and said nothing. As Mrs. B continued to berate Mr. B about his passivity and inability to take a stance against his domineering mother who never accepted Mrs. B, the therapist crawled toward the door and started pounding. This finally got Mrs. B's attention. She stopped and asked what the therapist's behavior was supposed to mean. The therapist redirected the question and asked if she could come up with an answer. After a short pause, Mrs. B reluctantly turned to her husband, "Did I really make you feel this bad?" Mr. B nodded, and said, "All the damn time!"

The therapist then engaged the couple to explore the hurt feelings connected with not being accepted by Mr. B's family. It was partly this unacceptance that created stereotyping and a mutual attacking of each others culture as it related to childrearing practices.

Paradoxical Intervention

In order to avoid marital conflicts, some intermarried couples adopt a "one-partner-taking-over" policy. Mary, an Irish Catholic, took seriously her Catholic commitment to do all within her power to rear the children Catholic. In addition to insuring that their son, John, got the proper Catholic education at church and at home, Mary carefully screened his friends. On one occasion, Mary forbid John to join a baseball team because she did not want her son to be the only Catholic on the team. Mary's husband, Bob, is an Italian Catholic and disapproves of his wife's overcontrolling behavior, but he says nothing in order to preserve peace in the marriage. Bob instead withdraws from the family. He joined the Bass Fishing Club and became a weekend fisherman. Bob's detachment from the family necessitated his wife's taking full control of the home, including raising their son. Mary complained that she was tired of functioning as a single parent and John resented seldom seeing his father.

Mary's stress led to severe headaches. Her physician referred her to a family therapist when he realized that Mary's stress was caused mainly by her family problem. The therapist requested to see the couple conjointly, but Bob refused to come, claiming that Mary's headache had nothing to do with the marriage.

According to Mary, the couple married nine years ago. Mary's parents opposed the marriage using Bob's apathetic religious attitude as a strong reason. "And besides, Irish and Italian never mix well," Mary recalled her father saying when she asked his permission to marry Bob. Bob's parents were divorced, and he was never close to any of his family. According to Mary, Bob was very committed to the marriage, and he would never consider divorce for he resented his parents divorce when he was a child.

After the couple married, they had limited involvement with their extended families. Mary reasoned it was because her parents were devout Catholic, and they did not like Italian descendents. Mary felt extremely guilty that her marriage did not have her parents' blessing. She was not a devout Catholic herself when she was growing up, and she seemed surprised that she found herself placing so much emphasis on her own son growing up in a Catholic environment.

Mary admitted that she had seen two other therapists previously: one was a priest-therapist and the other one worked for a Catholic agency. When asked the reason behind her no longer seeing these therapists, Mary candidly replied that both therapists had advised her to let go of John and allow her husband to do some parenting too. Mary added, "They (therapists) mean well and they may have a point, but it is not easy for me to let John grow up like his father without a good religious upbringing."

Mary volunteered that her most current crisis was John's refusal to attend a summer camp sponsored by their Catholic church. John had attended the same camp last year and had been embarrassed by his mother's frequent visits.

The therapist validated Mary's devotion to her family, especially to her son. Instead of advising Mary not to interfere with John's camping trip (as the former therapists might have done), the therapist suggested to Mary that she telephone John at mutually agreed upon times.

When Mary discussed this with John, they agreed that Mary would call John once during the day and twice during the evening. When Mary happily related this plan to the therapist, he asked Mary if calling John just twice in the evening was enough. Mary replied immediately, "Of course not, but this is all John can agree to." The therapist then emphasized the importance of calling John on time so Mary would not interfere with his camp activities. Mary agreed.

Mary dutifully called John during the first three days of the trip. On the fourth day, she called the therapist for consultation.

When Mary saw the therapist, she looked dejected. She volunteered that over the past several days she had given serious thought to her behavior toward John and it affected her relationship with her husband.

Mary stated that John was already eight years old and could very nearly take care of himself. He did not need her calling him three times a day. "I guess I have to quit trying to please my father in making sure John grows up to be a good Catholic," added Mary.

An intermarried couple's definite role structure can be rigidified by previous life experiences, life-cycle changes, and their relationship with their family of origin. Frequently, those couples send the implicit message, "change our problem, but don't change us or anything else." From a systemic view, these couples are not really resisting as much as trying to preserve traits they feel are essential in maintaining the family unit.

In the above case, the husband was determined to minimize his cultural differences with his wife, whereas, the wife was determined to mold her son to be a good Catholic so that she would not disappoint her parents again as she had done when she married against their wishes. A couple's persistence in maintaining the old pattern of behavior may be so entrenched that standard therapeutic techniques are ineffective. Haley's (1976) paradoxical intervention is an appropriate technique for such "resistant" or "stuck" couples who minimize cultural differences and miscommunication to impede meaningful affectional exchanges.

Employing A Cotherapist Approach

In certain intermarried couple therapy situations, the presenting problem is accompanied by cultural explanations (usually negative in tone) given by one spouse for the behavior of the other. Throughout their marriage, the couple may have handled, more or less successfully, many cultural differences, such as race, language, and religion. Suddenly the couple seems impoverished, offering simplistic explanations that maximize their differences. When the person being blamed is a member of a foreign or minority subgroup, a first impression could suggest that the marital conflict replicates larger sociocultural tensions, such as racial or ethnic prejudice. A closer examination may reveal that other dysfunctional couple or family processes are at work, including the impending loss of a spouse through divorce or death. One spouse's stereotyping of the other spouse's culture may be indicative of more serious marital problems. To deal with situational prejudices which maximize the couple's cultural differences, a cotherapist approach can be useful in analyzing and rebuilding the marital relationship. The cotherapist approach with bicultural, bilingual, and bigender representation offers the following advantages in therapy with cross cultural couples.

1. It provides the intermarried couple with a comfortable and natural basis for joining. Such joining is essential due to the reluctance of some minority members who speak a different language and whose culture is different than the host community and that of the therapist. Each spouse can identify with a person from the team and feel that individual understands their needs culturally.

2. It provides a ready-made foundation for addressing the role of culture. Each therapist team member can readily focus on a cultural issue by underscoring the values, norms, or cultural relationship differences and the functions they serve in the present couple conflict.

3. It provides the couple with a role model for interaction and for problem solving (Norlin and Ho, 1974). Such a transcultural model is essential for it transcends the couple's ethnocentric model of problem assessment and problem solving. The couple will observe styles of behavior that work for the therapist team and see the skills demonstrated in the session.

4. It ensures continuity of therapy should one therapist become unavailable.

5. It avoids potential professional burnout, which is heightened when working with intermarried couples who speak different languages and whose cultural values differ from the therapist. A bicultural, bilingual and bigender therapist team is considered ideal. Bi-gender therapist teams can also provide similar advantages.

Potential disadvantages of the team approach in therapy with intermarried couples include disorganization and fragmentation, a great time commitment, therapist's conflicts (theoretical, training, experience), and excessive cost.

TECHNIQUES AND SKILLS IN RESOLVING CONFLICTS IN THE FAMILY LIFE-CYCLE AND EXTENDED FAMILY TIES

An individual's need for a positive sense of cultural identity and continuity with past traditions increases over the life-cycle (Gelfand and Kutzik, 1979). In an attempt to deny their differentness and their own identity conflicts as well as in an effort at mutual adaptation, intermarried couples are especially likely to abandon cultural rituals. Often, extended family support and acceptance is lost when an individual marries a person of a different race or ethnicity. Each family life-cycle or phase is affected by the response of the extended family to the intermarried couple. As a result, intermarried couples are often forced by their families or by social pressure to skip parts of each expected phase. Unresolved anger, hurt, and disappointment may contribute to family secrets, anniversary-related anxiety, or other couple conflicts or dysfunctions. The techniques and skills presented here can assist couples who experience family life-cycle conflicts and problems with extended families. They include therapy with the extended family, promoting interdependence, family obligation, and employing a therapist-helper.

Therapy with the Extended Family

When intermarried couple conflicts are related to parental disapproval or rejection, the therapist may intervene by interviewing the extended family. This can be a separate interview with the extended family or an interview conjointly with the intermarried couple, depending on the situation and the cooperation of the extended family. Therapy with the extended family requires the therapist be knowledgeable of the following dynamics which may impact extended family-intermarried couple conflicts.

Many parents disapprove of intermarriage because of the prevalent and persistent fear that people who are visibly different or speak a different language may think and behave differently. Such perceived differences can cause parents uncertainty and anxiety. Parents may feel they do not know how to interact with others who are different. The partner of different race or ethnicity may feel awkward in interacting with in-laws and may feel the in-laws have less respect for them. Moreover, friends and associates of parents may insinuate to parents that their children's intermarriage is a clear reflection of their inadequate guidance and poor childrearing.

Such parents are likely to see their children's intermarriage as an act of disobedience or defiance as proscribed by ethnic and racial teachings. When such disobedience is displayed publicly (as it is in the case of intermarriage) many parents suffer disappointment and extreme humiliation. The hurt and suffering of parents may be so real and intense that they interpret their children's decision to intermarry as a public insult and rejection of them. When parents are struggling with their own wounds, they are unable to listen to and be empathic toward their children's needs. It is important that the therapist be empathic to the parents' hurt. Listening to the parents and giving them an opportunity to vent their anger is often a necessary step in the therapy process. Afterwards, parents may then be able to discuss the situation more objectively.

Some parents' hostility toward their children's intermarriage is aggravated by the pain of the parent-child separation process which *every* parent has to face. If the parent-child relationship prior to intermarriage has been positive, parents often feel considerable ambivalence and reluctance in letting go of their son or daughter. If the relationship has been negative, parents may feel regret and even guilt when they are informed that their son or daughter is leaving them for another person of a different race or ethnicity. These parents may feel they have forced their children into intermarriage. Obviously, such parents need assurance, preferably from their children, that the decision to intermarry is not a sign of disapproval or rejection of them. These parents also need reassurance that their children will continue to need them and to desire a positive relationship with them.

Finally, some parents' disapproval or rejection of a child who intermarries is generated by their own marital discord. Their conscious or unconscious effort to control their children's marriage is their continued attempt to avoid dealing directly with their own marriage. Unless the parents express a desire to work on their own marital problems, a therapist should avoid telling the parents that they need marital therapy. Instead, the therapist should focus on getting the parents to help their child and accept his or her intermarriage.

Promoting Interdependence and Family Obligation

Intermarried couples, especially those involving a spouse from a collectivist culture, greatly value what others, especially family members, think of them. An individual's worth is dependent upon how well she or he gets along with other family members. As a child, one is expected to comply with parental and social authority. The parent has the responsibility and obligation to perpetuate the family's "good" name. A therapist can challenge the parents of the intermarried couple to fulfill their obligation and maintain the family unit. In the case of husband and wife conflict, the therapist can ask both spouses to refrain from expecting favors from each other and instead challenge them to render good deeds or favors to each other. The same challenge can be directed to an extended family member who disapproves of the intermarriage. Each member of the family has an obligation to make the family a harmonious unit.

When parents of an intermarried couple resist therapy, the therapist can gently remind them or other authority figures that their familial role as elder carries with it educative duties to younger family members. Unless they can practice self-control, they may fail as a positive role model (obligation) to the younger members of the family.

The therapist's warm acceptance of the client can make the client feel he or she should be mutually accepting of the therapist. The therapist can use the client's feelings of obligation to return favors, to challenge the client to follow instructions or directives, and to help the couple resolve its problem.

Employing a Therapist-Helper

If the intermarried couple exhibits cultural shock, language difficulty, the distrust and unfamiliarity with the concept of couple therapy, poor self-other differentiation, and a resistance to therapy, the traditional therapist-couple therapeutic approach may not be feasible. Instead, the strategic use of a therapist-helper, who is a trusted friend of the couple or an extended family member, may be required to help the couple solve its problem. The therapist-helper approach is indicated when the couple is persistently uncooperative or too emotional and when there is a definite language barrier between the therapist and the couple or with one spouse. In addition to being the last resort by which some intermarried couples can be helped, the therapist-helper approach provides the couple with a normal approach to problem solving.

Intermarriage involves individuals from two different cultures and sometimes with different native languages. The therapist-helper ideally needs to be bicultural, bilingual, and accepted by both spouses. This helper may already be a trusted friend of the intermarried. The procedure may be introduced to the couple as a way for the therapist to get some needed help because she or he has been ineffective thus far in assisting the couple. In that way, the therapist can take a one-down position and encourage the couple to work harder with the helper to resolve their problems.

It is often necessary to explicate the temporary, consultative role of the therapist-helper in order to make the helper's involvement clear to the couple. The issue of confidentiality may also need to be delineated. Additionally, the therapist-helper needs regular coaching and supervision from the therapist. The following case example illustrates the use of the therapist-helper technique.

Mary, a Caucasian, was upset because over the past month she had hardly seen her husband, Vin, a Vietnamese, and their three-month-old son. Vin got off work earlier than Mary, so he picked up their son from the nursery and went to his parents' home. His parents openly criticized Mary for returning to work right after the baby was born. Although Vin realized the financial necessity of Mary's working, he still felt guilty that his parents' desires were unmet. His uncertainty about his priorities, whether to please his parents or his wife, caused him considerable personal misery and threatened his relationship with his wife and young son. As the couple was struggling with their problems, in-laws from both families contended that because of their cultural differences, the couple should never have married.

Vin started having closer interaction with his parents after his son was born. Vin lately had developed colitis, which the physician attributed to psychological stress. Despite Mary's constant plea for Vin to enter into couple therapy, Vin rejected the idea. "Therapist speaks your language and belongs to your culture; he cannot help me," complained Vin.

When Mary related to the therapist her husband's reluctance to enter into therapy, he asked Mary if the couple had a mutual friend whom both trusted. Mary responded that Vin always liked his English instructor who was Caucasian, but was married to a Vietnamese man. This same person had been the English instructor of Vin's parents and had an excellent rapport with them. The therapist asked Mary to consult with her husband about the possibility of using their friend, the English instructor, for a therapist-helper. Vin agreed. The therapist gave Mary directions on how to approach their friend. Their friend agreed to meet with the therapist for further consultation regarding her role as a therapist-helper.

The new therapist-helper saw the couple for three sessions. As a result, the couple began to communicate better, and both spouses realized the need for greater intimacy, mutual involvement in childrearing, and less control and influence from in-laws, especially Vin's parents. Despite the new understanding and agreement, Vin still had problems in dealing with his parents who wanted closer involvement with their grandson. They criticized Vin for losing his cultural roots and respect for them as parents.

The therapist then coached the therapist-helper to talk with Vin's parents. She explained that Vin almost had a nervous breakdown because of loyalty conflicts between his parents and his wife. Vin's parents were very concerned about their son's health and they asked the helper what they could do. The therapist coached the helper in how to suggest to Vin's parents that they make fewer demands on him. Additionally, Vin and his wife were helped to improve their attitudes and relationship with Vin's parents. As Mary got to spend more time with her son, she was more willing to visit her in-laws. This pleased Vin's parents a great deal. As a result, Vin's health began to improve. Therapy was terminated after two months. The therapist only saw Mary once, and there was no direct contact between the therapist and Vin and Vin's parents. The therapist-helper saw the couple six sessions, which ranged from forty-five minutes to two hours per session. She also spent six one-hour consultative sessions with the therapist.

TECHNIQUES AND SKILLS IN RESOLVING IDIOSYNCRATIC PROBLEMS IN INTERMARRIAGE

Generally, conflicts or problems between the intermarried are attributed directly or indirectly to their cultural differences. However, there are times when intermarried couple problems are caused by idiosyncratic problems on the part of one or both partners. Examples of idiosyncratic problems include personality fragmentation, dissociative behavior, rapid mood swing, violent behavior, and alcohol or drug abuse. How an individual experiences such problems to some extent is culturally determined. Idiosyncratic problems often cause self-destructive behavior and are detrimental to close marital or family relationships. Four techniques and skills are presented to assist the intermarried couple in resolving such conflicts. These include diagnosing the idiosyncratic problem, specifying the therapeutic goals, working through, and personality and marital integration.

Diagnosing the Idiosyncratic Problem

In diagnosing an idiosyncratic problem, the therapist should determine that the marital problem is not caused externally, despite the fact it is the *interpersonal* marital problem that motivates the couple to seek help. It is also important for the therapist to establish that the problem is not cultural or transitory in nature, because these type problems are frequently associated with newly arrived immigrants. The following case illustrates an intermarried couple's problem that is correctly diagnosed as idiosyncratic.

When Ferendo, a Mexican-American divorced man in his forties, met his second wife-to-be, Theresa, a Caucasian, he experienced a unique feeling of understanding and closeness. Although they were of different races, their ideas, tastes, and interests were so similar that "they could have been twins," according to Ferendo. He admired her greatly, as she did him. Both loved partying and going out together in public. However, even before their marriage, Ferendo began to have periods when he felt completely disinterested in Theresa and could not understand why he was with her. These feelings later caused sexual incompatibility in the marriage. Theresa's persistent approach made Fernando want to disappear completely. The couple exchanged negative cultural stereotypes to justify their behavior. Fernando's episodes of disillusionment and denigration of Theresa increased after marriage and led the couple to seek marital therapy.

Ferendo's father had died when he was four, and he had a traumatic relationship with his mother, who was emotionally unstable. Ferendo also had suffered from marked swings in his feelings toward his first wife. In the ensuing marital therapy, Ferendo's disturbance was very profound and resistant to change. However, he agreed to enter into individual therapy and insisted that he would do whatever was needed to in order to save his marriage.

This marriage problem was accurately diagnosed as an idiosyncratic problem. This couple did not experience sociocultural conflict or ecological deficits. They had a good income, good occupations, and communicated well when the husband was not feeling empty and worthless and projecting these feelings onto his wife. Both reported having good relationships with their in-laws and the majority of the time, they really enjoyed being married to each other.

Since the couple desired to stay married, it was important that while the husband was being seen in individual therapy that couple therapy also continue. Couple therapy was employed to help both the husband and the therapist assess, treat, and integrate his personality and was essential to a continuous, stable couple relationship. If individual therapy with the husband was employed exclusively, the wife would be left out of the couple relationship process. She might sabotage her husband's therapy. If the husband achieved progress in individual therapy without involving the wife in the process, the couple's relationship might run the risk of further fragmentation.

Specification of Therapeutic Goals

The above case illustrates, in extreme form, the self object-function (Kohut, 1984, p. 52) of twinship, mirroring and idealization. These play an important part in a happy, satisfactory relationship. The husband's oscillations between feelings of twinship and estrangement and between feelings of idealization and denigration were characteristic of an individual suffering from early disturbances in their relationship to significant others (Finkelstein, 1987; Kernberg, 1976). The specific goals in individual therapy with the husband were to:

1. identify the personality splitting (twinship and estrangement, idealization and denigration),
2. integrate the personality splitting, and
3. engage in a continuous, stable, intimate couple relationship.

Working Through

The therapist engages the client to share his or her early traumatic experiences. Intense feelings are expressed by reliving the original events (surrounding the death of the client's father and his rejection by his unempathic mother) in the presence of the therapist who empathizes with the client in a safe and supportive atmosphere. Conflicting emotions, such as idealization and denigration, are worked through and resolved in order to provide a new perspective about the trauma. Transference issues with the therapist and spouse need to be identified and understood. It is important that the client's spouse be included in the "working through" of the transference issues so that the client will learn to differentiate between his wife and his mother or other "past abusers."

Personality and Couple Integration

The therapist assists the client to learn new coping mechanisms which will help the unified personality to function effectively and prevent splitting. These coping mechanisms include learning cognitive and experiential techniques to facilitate the acceptance and resolution of internal conflicts (splitting), learning new skills for the reduction and management of stress, and improving couple communication skills that promote the appropriate and effective expression of needs and feelings. Conjoint marital therapy is vital at this stage. It facilitates the client's and the couple's learning of new communication skills and sociocultural expectations. It stabilizes the changed couple system and reduces marital or family crises which could foster new splitting.

The object-relation concepts provide a therapist with an understanding of the deeper reasons for intermarried couple conflicts that go beyond cultural differences. The couple's conflicts and resistance to change, irregardless of cultural differences, can be understood as consequences of idiosyncratic problems of relatedness, of deficiencies in self object functioning, and of conflicts between the relationship goals and individual goals. By understanding these reasons, the therapist can help the intermarried couple change on a deeper level, thereby helping them to achieve a more lasting improvement in their relationship.

TECHNIQUES AND SKILLS IN EVALUATION AND TERMINATION

The evaluation and termination of intermarried couple therapy has an important cultural aspect. The task here is to reconnect and restore the couple to their larger world. As the engagement stage, the couple's original life strategy is again validated, along with the changes and modifications introduced in the therapy. For new adaptive strategies to improve the couple relationship, they must work after and apart from the interaction with the therapist. These strategies must be truly owned culturally by the intermarried couple.

Couple therapy with the intermarried is a continuous process that starts slowly and ends slowly. However, how the therapy ends depends also on the racial or ethnic composition of the couple. For example, the Irish spouse may wish to end the therapy abruptly, without clear acknowledgement of having been helped, and without wishing to "spoil" the therapist with praise. British Americans may also end abruptly when "business" is done rather than "process" their separation with the therapist. A Jewish spouse may end therapy unwillingly, complaining of the inadequate "depth" of emotional insight yet sustaining the improved behavior.

Spouses from collectivist cultures usually are considerate of the therapist's time and efforts. They prefer not to burden the therapist but to terminate therapy prematurely.

Considering the cultural complexity of intermarried couples and the different reasons behind their seeking therapeutic help, evaluation of therapy progress should be guided by three types of outcome goals. First are the *intermediate* outcomes that contribute to or create a climate for continued therapy. Some intermarried couples, because of situational stress and language deficiency, will only allow the therapist to help them with some basic needs. When this is accomplished, therapy terminates.

Second are the *instrumental* outcomes. When achieved, these are assumed to lead to the achievement of the ultimate outcome without further therapy. Once these needs are met, the couple can go on with the task of repairing intimacy bonds within the marriage. Third are *ultimate* outcomes, which constitute the primary reason for which therapy was undertaken. Examples of these outcome goals include the marital relationship, childrearing practices, in-law relationships, and physical illnesses that are caused by marital stresses.

Because of their "present orientation" and, at times, language deficiency, clients from collectivist cultures may not verbally express the progress they make in therapy. They may not want to recall the painful past that brought them in for therapy. Neither will they wish to anticipate future problems they feel are irrelevant to the present situation.

The termination process with intermarried couples should take into consideration the couple's concept of time and space in a relationship. Some couples may never want to end a good relationship, and they learn to respect and love the therapist as a member of their family. It is important that a therapist be comfortable with this element of cultural and human inclusiveness and make termination a natural and gradual process.

The above discussion concludes the presentation of relevant techniques and skills in therapy with intermarried couples in the problem-solving stage. Chapter 6 will be devoted to a presentation of techniques and skills that relate to specific therapy modalities and issues with intermarried couples.

Chapter 6

SPECIFIC THERAPY MODALITIES AND ISSUES

Marital therapy with intermarried couples presents unique challenges, as discussed in previous chapters. Helping couples of different race or ethnicity also requires special considerations and strategies in other therapeutic modalities.

This chapter explores three different types of modalities with intermarried couples: premarital therapy, divorce therapy, and single-parent therapy. The chapter concludes with a special section on intermarried couple therapy for military personnel. This book has been written not only to be informative, but to be practical and useful to those in the classroom and those in the field. A large percentage of intermarried couples are associated with the military and often share common problems and needs. We trust the information presented here will be particularly helpful.

Premarital Therapy with Intermarried Couples

Sylvia, an attractive nineteen-year-old Jewish female, walked into the therapist's office with tears in her eyes. As she sat down, she immediately asked, "Why are parents, especially fathers, so unreasonable?" She explained that her Orthodox father opposed her engagement to John, a popular Irish Catholic boy in her sophomore sociology class. I can't understand what the fuss is about. Both of us are white, from middle-class families, and are liberal minded adults who understand and respect each other's religion and ethnicity, complained Sylvia. The therapist empathized with Sylvia about how disappointed she was by her father's objections, and he asked her the reason she was sharing this information with him professionally. Sylvia replied that as a compromise with her father, she agreed to see a marital therapist and that the therapist's own intermarried status was the primary reason she chose him. If anybody can understand my situation, I thought that you'd be the one," added Sylvia.

Taking advantage of this instant rapport, the therapist asked Sylvia if she would be willing to take the Marriage Potentials Inventory the therapist had developed especially for couples planning to marry or who are already in an intermarriage (see Appendix A—Marriage Potentials Inventory). The therapist explained to Sylvia that the purpose of the inventory was to help her assess and better understand her relationship with her fiancee, an important step in resolving the impasse with her father. Sylvia displayed no hesitancy in taking the inventory and commented afterward that it helped her consider some points which she had not thought of previously. To encourage Sylvia to feel free to discuss her feelings regarding her relationship with her fiancee, the therapist commented on the several relationship categories in which she scored high. The therapist then directed her to examine the Religious/Cultural Orientation Category. Sylvia realized that despite her willingness to respect her fiancee's Catholic belief (her score on this item was 4 on a scale of 5), she had not actually learned about Catholicism (her score on this item was 2), nor did she believe in the need for active involvement in her fiancee's religion (her score on this item was also 2). Sylvia was equally surprised when she discovered that her score on questions pertaining to raising children was also low. "As a matter of fact, John never shared with me the requirements of the Catholic church regarding raising children," complained Sylvia. The therapist suggested that it would be helpful if she discussed with John this matter and other issues concerning each other's religions and ethnic orientations.

Sylvia returned with John for the second therapy session, explaining that she could not discuss emotional issues with John alone without getting into an argument. John was straightforward in explaining that he planned to marry within the dictates of his church. He had felt all along that when Sylvia took the marriage preparation instructions, she would see the value of the Catholic religion, turn to it, and their problems would be solved. Sylvia was very angry about John's statements and assured him that she would never become a Catholic. One week later Sylvia telephoned the therapist and reported that her engagement to John was called off indefinitely.

Mary, a 21-year-old Caucasian, came to see the therapist for therapy upon her mother's recommendation. The mother felt that Mary's father was facing a nervous breakdown as a result of Mary's relationship with a young Thai man. Mary was a college senior majoring in liberal arts and was contemplating marrying and moving to Thailand upon graduation.

After a few sessions, Mary was still unconvinced that her marriage to a Thai and their living in Thailand would be very different from marrying a man of the same race and cultural background. The therapist arranged for Mary to visit a Thai couple, who in turn, introduced Mary to several other Thai families in the community. After a few visits with them, Mary realized that she might not be comfortable with the role women assume in Thai society and that she surely did not wish her children brought up as Buddhists. Furthermore, Mary realized that despite her future husband's understanding of her cultural background, his family, relatives, and friends might not treat her the same way he did. Mary became more uncertain about her marital plans, although she did not totally rule out marriage with a Thai. The therapist encouraged her and her Thai boyfriend to take time to consider their decision.

These two cases reflect the unique nature of premarital therapy with couples from different ethnicities and races and some of the specific therapeutic skills required to respond to the couple's special needs. The following four steps merit the attention of the therapist who prepares individuals for intermarriage: (1) evaluation of client's motivation, (2) evaluation of client's expectations, (3) enabling the client to anticipate future benefits as well as potential difficulties, and (4) evaluation of client's own strengths and couple's compatibility.

Evaluation of Client's Motivation. Various reasons motivate people to intermarry, these have been described in Chapter 1 of this book. Sylvia's incentive to marry John was partly due to romantic love and partly due to her struggle to establish a self-identity. In seeking emancipation, she was rejecting her parents' religious beliefs. With therapy, she was able to face realities which were quite different from her assumptions and expectations. Despite her relatively weak religious commitment to Judaism, she was not ready for her children to be of the Catholic faith, which she knew almost nothing about. Her ability to face this reality helped her think beyond her idealistic, romantic feelings toward her fiancee.

As a liberal arts student, Mary's attraction to her Thai boyfriend was motivated by her fascination with new experiences and other cultures. Once the unexpected realities were explored and partially experienced, Mary was able to become more realistic and in touch with her true needs and natural attachment to her cultural environment.

The therapist, in helping the individual assess his or her motives, needs to be empathic and nonjudgmental. To explore what brought the client in for consultation helps the therapist assess the level of resistance to therapy which the client is experiencing. Specifically, the therapist should identify with the client's disappointment, hurt, distrust, and any guilt feelings toward parents who oppose the intermarriage. Moreover, the therapist should not imply that the intermarriage will not work. Instead, the therapist's role should be limited to that of an empathic listener enabling the client to explore openly and fully his or her own motives for intermarriage. Any direct advice given by the therapist at this time may be interpreted by the client as coercion and, therefore, strongly defended against.

Evaluation of Client's Expectations. Sylvia's original expectation that she and her fiancee would accept each other's religion was challenged by the therapist's use of the Marriage Potential Inventory as a tool to help her face reality. Mary's contemplation of interracial marriage was based on an illusion. What her partner should be like instead of what he was, a Thai who would be living in Thailand. Mary's illusion made it difficult for her to realize all the ramifications of living in a different cultural environment. The therapist sensed Mary's unrealistic expectations and exposed her to a "next-to real" cultural environment to help her face reality.

In helping a client close the gap between expectation and reality, a therapist will find the following points particularly useful: a woman's attitude toward her own social position and toward man; the dissimilarity in cultural attitudes toward the status and role of women and the degree of restriction placed by custom upon their behavior; attitudes toward authority; organization of the family with respect to relatives and in-laws; and morality and aesthetics inherent in each culture, ethnicity, and religion. Additionally, the therapist should encourage the couple contemplating intermarriage to read more about each other's culture and to associate more with one another's family, relatives, and friends. A rundown of actual wedding plans, future living arrangements, and expected cultural, religious and social activities will sometimes reveal potential problems.

Enabling the Client to Anticipate Future Complications and Difficulties. Despite the usefulness and the necessity of trying to anticipate future complications and difficulties, intermarried couples often resist and guard against this in premarital therapy. The therapist should be sensitive to this and not proceed with the exploration without first developing a trusting relationship with the couple. To highlight potential difficulties in the intermarriage, the therapist may use the Marriage Potentials

Inventory. In Sylvia's case, taking the inventory as a routine part of the therapeutic process enabled her to discover many areas in her relationship with her fiancee that she had previously neglected. Her sudden awareness of her lack of preparation in certain areas aided the therapist's efforts to help her acknowledge potential problems.

Another way to help a couple anticipate future problems is to introduce them to real-life experiences of an already intermarried couple, as was done in the case of Mary.

Evaluation of Client's Personal Strengths and the Couple's Compatibility. Since intermarriages have additional benefits as well as additional sources of potential conflict, it is safe to assume that individuals involved in intermarriage will need exceptional ego and emotional strength and a high degree of compatibility as a couple in order to make their marriage a success. The strength needed refers to one's ability to make sound decisions and handle stress. Compatibility refers to a couple's ability to communicate effectively, to solve problems, and to achieve common goals. When a husband and wife have significant personal strengths and a high degree of compatibility, their marriage is likely to endure and eventually overcome all sorts of limitations and discriminations.

If Mary and Sylvia had possessed great ego strengths and were compatible with their partners, they might have been able to build successful intermarriages. To do so, Sylvia and her partner would have needed to devise a creative plan to resolve their religions, family, and other problems. In the case of Mary, she and her Thai boyfriend would have to decide such things as whether to stay in this country or live outside Thailand. If they should decide to marry and reside in Thailand, their Thai relatives could help by not imposing their attitudes and Thai customs on the couple, or Mary could wholly embrace the Thai culture.

To assess an individual's ability to succeed in an intermarriage, a therapist needs to review the client's past and present adjustment patterns, educational and work history, expectations in marriage, interpersonal relationships, relationship with family of origins, and coping mechanisms, including flexibility and adaptability to new environments (Ho, 1984). To assess the couple's compatibility, inquiry can be made as to how the couple handles differences. Are they able to reach a compromise acceptable to both or does one always give in and then resent it? How often and how intensely does the couple quarrel? Does quarreling result in better understanding and more acceptance or does it result in blocking off certain touchy issues that are no longer discussed? Do they respect each other? Do they feel supported, valued, and appreciated for what they are? Lastly, the therapist should explore with the couple whether their parents support the marriage. How do they plan to cope with their parents or relatives who are not supportive of their marriage? The relationship categories of communication and conflict resolution on the Marriage Potentials Inventory are intended to sensitize the therapist and the couple to the couple's compatibility.

Divorce Therapy with Intermarried Couples

There is a dearth of literature pertaining to divorce among the intermarried. Limited findings in the literature leave doubt as to whether intermarriages are more or less stable than same race marriages (Crester and Leon, ed., 1982). Some researchers suggest that intermarriage between Blacks and Whites is relatively stable (Golden, 1959; Monahan, 1970). Others raise questions about how this could be possible in our society where special pressures are focused on such intermarriages and where such marriages were actually illegal until 1967.

The most recent study by Rankin and Maneker (Everett, ed., 1988) based on a 10 percent random sample of all divorce cases in California in 1977 helps to resolve some of these conflicting views. Marriages which involve black husbands and white wives differ in several aspects from same-race marriages and differ somewhat from white husband-black wife marriages. Not only are they shorter in duration from marriage to final divorce decrees, they have fewer children or none at all; spouses rank relatively high in education. They involve relatively few teenagers partly because of the relatively high percentage of black husbands who have been previously married. In addition, black husbands, in black-white marriages, are less likely to file for divorce than husbands in the same race or white-black marriages. While the higher educational level for husbands and wives may be associated with successful marriages in the general population, this appears less likely in black-white marriages. Educational advantages may serve to bring mixed marital partners together, but they may not serve to hold them together. In fact, more highly educated white wives may be in a better position to terminate an unsatisfactory marriage. There is also a lack of parental incentive to hold these marriages together because such couples have fewer, or no children.

While there is no specific, applicable literature on intermarriage involving other ethnic minority groups, there are some understandings as to how each minority reacts to the divorce experience. Among many minority groups, divorce is regarded in a more socially acceptable light because of the following factors: the breakdown of extended family ties, high unemployment, unmet physical and economic needs, poor physical and mental health, high rate of alcoholism and attempted suicides. American Indians' and Blacks' traditional respect for individuality, a person's right to make his own decision, and their strong belief in noninterference make divorce have a limited negative stigma. Conversely, Asian Americans consider divorce a family disgrace. The strong Catholic influence upon Hispanics, Irish Americans, and Italian Americans contributes to their relatively low divorce rate. The attitudes of the intermarried couples comprised of different ethnic groups toward divorce greatly affect the decision for divorce and the adjustment of the divorcees. For instance, American Indians and Blacks usually have extended families who offer unconditional acceptance of divorce. This greatly facilitates the adjustment of the divorcees. An Asian or Hispanic divorcee may risk ostracism from the extended family or the Catholic church, thus making the adjustment more traumatic and difficult. Most minority individuals, especially those with traditional orientations, are not familiar with legal divorce proceedings. Those who decide to end their marriages may not wish to discuss it with a therapist whose expertise is unknown to them. Hence, divorce therapy usually is indicated after the client has medical treatment for physical symptoms, or after the client has established a trusting relationship with the therapist through different presenting problems. Because divorce is a very serious step for the intermarried individual or couple, the following recommendations are suggested to ensure that clients receive appropriate help and services.

Exploring Divorce Experiences and Consequences. Given that divorce is regarded as socially unacceptable among some intermarried couples, especially those whose parents disapproved, a therapist needs to help the client anticipate the possible feelings of guilt, failure or ostracism he or she will face. The therapist needs to access the client's strength to withstand these painful and potential punitive consequences without resorting to physical maladies. For couples experiencing constant physical abuse or prolonged emotional sufferings due to unresolved conflicts, the therapist may introduce an analogous concept, such as temporary separation, as a means to dilute the tension between a husband and wife. The therapist must be cautious due to the intermarried couple's unique situation and different concept about divorce. The premature introduction of the idea of divorce may hasten the termination process of therapy or it may render disservice to clients whose problems would be compounded by the lack of familial and social support resulting from divorce.

The final decision for dissolving the intermarriage usually entails the husband/wife shifting from a collateral to an individualistic orientation. This may cause great pain and uncertainty and it can temporarily immobilize a person's normal functioning. For individuals who have experienced a great deal of rejection and criticism in the past, the divorce experience can reactivate a repressed negative self-image, causing the individual to feel unloved or unworthy (Kohut, 1972).

Furthermore, the emotional vacuum created by divorce can throw the divorcee into a state of total frustration and desperation. This crisis can be compounded by the fact that the divorcee has no prior knowledge or experience in utilizing community health and social services. The role of the therapist is to assess the client's needs and act quickly to help the client resolve them.

Providing the Client with Legal and Social Support. If divorce is the alternative chosen by the client, the therapist's role is to provide the client with the best possible legal assistance by helping secure a matrimonial lawyer who is not only proficient in divorce proceedings but also is sensitive to the client's cultural orientation and background. Divorce can be especially traumatic if the decision to end the marriage is not mutual and if the divorced partner (usually a female) has no employable skills. Further, the divorcee may be left with several children to support. The therapist's first task is to assess the extent of the divorcee's extended family support system. Should the divorcee's extended family system be unavailable due to geographical distance or emotional cutoff, the therapist should help the client secure a support system consisting of close friends. The divorcee also needs to be informed of public health and social agencies that can provide temporary assistance for her and the family.

Whenever the divorcee is temporarily incapacitated by the divorce, the therapist needs to assume the executive role of the family. This involves finding a means to meet the family's basic needs and providing the divorcee with concrete and emotional support. Concrete support may include transporting her to a health clinic and helping her food shop. Some clients, during this critical stage become very emotional and highly dependent. The therapist should anticipate and be comfortable with the client's dependency, while at the same time helping her to become interdependent and work with other support groups.

Postdivorce Adjustment. Considering the social isolation a divorced individual faces, plus the extended family isolation many intermarried individuals experience, simply coping after divorce can be very traumatic, especially to those individuals struggling with acculturation and the English language. Once the critical stage of divorce is stabilized and the family's basic needs are being met, the therapist's next task is to engage the client in assessing her emotional feelings about the previous spouse. It is to be expected that many intermarried individuals have invested a great deal in their marriage and they find it difficult to acknowledge the finality of the divorce. The former spouse, after all, remains her children's father. Her children's conscious and unconscious fantasy or maneuvers in getting their father back into the family do not help the mother cope with divorce or the feeling of loss. The therapist's role is to sensitize the client to the possible negative effects this emotional tie may have on her and her children if it prevails. Such indecision and unfinished business with her ex-spouse can also prevent her from entering into a new relationship enriching to her and her children.

Some divorced individuals, especially those who are from a collectivist culture, may have difficulty in assuming new roles after divorce, especially the role of the breadwinner and disciplinarian for the children. To compensate for their guilt and to save face and reaffirm their decision to divorce, some divorced individuals are reluctant to seek and receive help from relatives and close friends. Some relatives and close friends may not agree with the client's decision to divorce and withdraw their support and sympathy for the client. The therapist's role is to be a systems broker between the client and her relatives and close friends. When relatives and close friends of the divorcee choose not to be involved with the client, the therapist's task is to help the client secure new support systems. Preferably with other divorcee's who have shared similar experiences.

Single-Parent Therapy

Despite the fact that there is little in the literature on single parents who one time were intermarried, most investigations reach remarkably similar conclusions, suggesting that single parents generally experience a complex array of problems. In particular, these include a wide range of financial and social difficulties which, in turn, can cause single parents to be psychologically less well adjusted than their counterparts from intact marriages (Burden, 1986). In contrast to those from intact families, single parents are more depressed, more anxious, have lower self-images, and are less satisfied with their lives (Fine et al., 1985). Similarly, Weiss (1979) found that following separation many single parents were overwhelmed with their increased role responsibilities and experienced a pervasive sense of loneliness.

Literature reports that most children experience the transition into a single parent home (especially after divorce) as a stressful live event and exhibit short-term developmental disruptions, behavioral disorders, and emotional distress (Hetherington, 1981). In a clinical study of biracial children whose parents were divorced, Teicher (1979) proposed a series of hypotheses: (1) children would identify with the parent perceived as less socially depreciated; (2) problems of sexual identify would occur with greater frequency among children whose same-sexed parent is different from them in racial characteristics; (3) problems of sexual identity would also occur with greater frequency among children who themselves depreciate the racial characteristics of the same-sexed parent or who perceive that the opposite-sexed parent depreciates the child's or the spouse's racial characteristics; (4) the greater the child's problem of racial identification, the greater the problem of sexual identification; (5) biracial children have fewer problems of racial identity if they live in a community of mixed marriages, than if they live in one predominantly racial community.

The first year of single parenthood requires adjustment in many facets of one's lifestyle, including one's relationship with parents and other relatives. During this transition period the woman may need to rely more heavily on her family for emotional and material aid, but reactions of family members may compound the problems she experiences. A recent study by Wagner (1988) discomfirms the assertion that Mexican-American extended families have greater tolerance of unconventional lifestyle such as divorce and that they are more emotionally supportive than Anglo extended families. Under normal circumstances the family network of the collectivist culture may be quite supportive, but when behaviors occur that violate the norms, such as intermarriage or divorce, the network may exert negative sanctions and become a source of stress.

Available evidence indicates that single parents of intermarriage are experiencing more stress than that normally associated with divorce and being a new single parent. Three techniques and skills are presented to assist therapists who work with single parents of intermarriage. These include: (1) mobilizing the support system; (2) assisting the single parent to restructure the family, and (3) assisting the single parent to define and meet personal needs.

Mobilizing the Support System. In view of the close-knit family ties of the collectivist cultures, a divorcee seldom finds herself taking care of children without at the same time receiving some means of assistance from relatives or close friends. Again, the single parent's relationship with her own extended family will play a crucial role in whether the extended family supports the single parent.

In a situation where divorce is too much a stigma for the extended family members, the therapist's task is to be a systems broker between the client and her relatives. Additionally, the therapist needs to sensitize the relatives to the various needs of a single parent who may be reluctant to seek help from them actively. The needs of a single parent obviously are the primary concern, but a therapist should never lose sight of the fact that the single parent's relatives also feel ambivalent and may have unmet needs. The therapist needs to be supportive and patient with the relatives who may choose to ventilate their disappointment, anger, and resentment toward the single parent. The therapist's accepting attitude toward the single parent can be a consoling force to the relatives who may have feared others would attach a stigma to the divorce.

When there are no extended family ties available, the therapist should help the single parent establish new ties by contacting church groups, ethnic minority service agencies, neighbors, or friends. Literature on minority single parents suggests that the friend network becomes more important over time (Halem, 1982). The friend network becomes a surrogate family for many single mothers, in some ways replacing familial functions. The initial choice for many single parents is to move in with their own parents, but this coexistence is usually a temporary phase that ends when the woman is more financially secure. She will also become more independent when she establishes an alternative network of friends.

Assisting the Single Parent in Restructuring the Family and in Proper Parenting. The absence of the father from the spousal system and from the family as a whole requires family renegotiation and a restructuring of the family system boundary (Minuchin, 1974). The Asian and Hispanic American hierarchical role structure by age and sex can easily place the oldest male child in the father role. The traditional closeness of the mother-child relationship should not be automatically assumed to be enmeshment. However, if the mother-child relationship excludes other siblings or extended family members, there is a concern as to whether the present relationship is conducive to the normal development and optimum functioning of the family (Ho, 1987).

To help a single parent function effectively, the therapist is advised to assess if daily household tasks such as cooking, cleaning, children attending schools, and so on are properly taken care of. In addition, the therapist needs to assess if the mother is effective in providing emotional nurturance for her children. Interracial or interethnic children continue to develop identities regardless of their parents' marital status. If the parents' divorce was not properly resolved, interracial children often receive conflicting messages about their own identity from parents and family members on both sides. White parents may not be able to accept the fact that society will not define their children as "white" and may give them mixed messages about their skin color and nonwhite appearance (Benson, 1981; Lyles, 1985). Some parents may handle the child's biracial identity through denial, simply refusing to discuss it or deal with it until a crisis occurs. Others assume a Pollyanna like attitude, behaving as if society were truly color-blind.

Depending on the mother's relationship with the extended family, some grandparents, aunts, uncles, and cousins may not accept the children as relatives after the parent's divorce. They may tease the children or make racist statements. It is important that the therapist encourage the single parent to clarify his or her own racial attitudes so that they can provide clear, consistent, and positive feedback to their children about both sides of their racial heritage. Under no circumstance should a single parent express negative feelings toward his or her children or view them as causes of their devalued social status or their failed marriage.

Assisting the Single Parent to Define and Meet Personal Needs. Women from collectivist cultures with their traditional devotion to motherhood sometimes find the adjustment to single-parenthood easier. Yet, the period of "singlehood" created by divorce can reactivate repressed, unresolved emotions and conflicts. Bowen's (1978) concept of differentiation of self is most applicable at this stage of therapy. The client at this time needs to assess where she has been and where she wishes to go. Close ties to the extended family are sources of strength. A single parent also needs to be aware of the fact that she is a separate person and has some control over how others treat her and how she acts and reacts to others. Intermarried individuals usually have given thought to the concept of self-differentiation when they consider marriage to others of different race or ethnicity. When the marriage fails, such an individual will increase his or her self doubt and may become excessively dependent. The therapist can encourage the single parent to reflect upon her strengths and future direction. She needs to evaluate her previous marital relationship and to derive some self-understanding about the kind of person she is, as well as the kind of persons she wishes to meet.

Whether a single parent can successfully meet her needs or not also depends on her children's cooperation and acceptance of her needs. Because most children of divorced parents harbor feelings of ambivalence, they fear their inattention and insensitivity may further alienate their mother. As a result, they become overly attentive and protective toward their mother. Their inability to let go also limits their mother's opportunity to be free and to attend to her own needs. A therapist's task then is to assist the children to understand their mother's needs and to help facilitate these needs whenever possible.

Military Intermarried Couple Therapy

Since World War II, nearly a quarter of a million marriages have been contracted between Asian women and U.S. servicemen overseas (Kim, 1981). These women have primarily come from countries where there is or has been a strong U.S. military presence—Japan, Korea, the Philippines, Vietnam, and Thailand. Asian spouses come from diverse socioeconomic backgrounds. Most come from undesirable and repressive social conditions such as economic disparity, war threats, traditional role rigidity, and intense extended family pressures to emigrate to the United States. Not only have the countries of these women been torn by wars and foreign domination including American military occupation, but also, Asian women have been socialized under the strong influences of Eastern philosophies and religions and cultural mores that represent vast cultural differences between East and West (Kim, 1981).

Many of these Asian women immigrate to the United States upon the reassignment of their American husbands. However, with the husband requesting repeated tour extensions, it is not unusual for these couples to remain overseas in the wife's native country for many years. As a result, the proportion of Asian-wife marriages at selective installations in the

Pacific ranges from between one-quarter to one-half of all service marriages (Orthner and Bowen, 1982). Whether or not the Asian wife remains in her native country or eventually returns with her husband to the U.S., these wives must acculturate to their new surroundings at a U.S. military installation and its associated hierarchy, traditions, regulations, and style of life.

It is likely that couples in the military face the same day-to-day problems as civilian couples. However, their problems are confounded with hardships inherent to the military—frequent moves, hectic and varying job schedules, and extended separations, all within the context of a seemingly insensitive rule-bound social system (Rodriguez, 1984). Potentially high-risk areas for military couples have been identified as alcohol abuse (Williams, 1984), lack of emotional expression among military husbands (Keith and Whitaker, 1984), and spouse abuse (Schwabe and Kaslow, 1984). A recent empirical study by Bowen and Henley (1987) also confirms that Asian wife marriages in the military experience greater disharmony in their nuclear or extended family relationships than other racial and ethnic couples with military husbands and civilian wives.

In an attempt to prevent failure and restore Asian wife marriage harmony in the military, Lee (1982) proposed three stages of psychological development for these Asian wives: the phases of cultural transition, accommodation, and transculturation.

During the early adjustment of the transitional phase, the degree of the Asian spouses' American cultural orientation, their personality, and their husbands' supportiveness will determine the effect of cultural and environmental change on the Asian spouse. The Asian spouse's proficiency in the English language also affects her adjustment. As Kim (1981) indicates that a major source of stress for Asian wives is often their inability to communicate effectively with significant others on the installation because of their lack of English proficiency. Additionally, the supportive role of the husband in providing both social access and companionship to the wife enhances the level of the couple's adjustment.

During this initial phase, both anticipating preparedness and a continuing supportive environment can provide an adjustment cushion for Asian-born spouses. Innovative cultural-sensitive programs, such as the Bride's School (Military Family, p. 5, 1982), are an excellent resource which aims to assist Asian wives and their American servicemen fiancees for the cultural transition the couples face upon returning to the U.S. The Bride School's major emphasis is on building confidence and knowledge among the young women who will be residing in the United States. In the early part of the school curriculum, basic knowledge such as how to use electrical appliances, opening a bank account, American style cooking, and family planning are included. The latter part of the curriculum includes general American ways of life, legal matters, public and private health systems.

To assist the Asian wife in the cultural transitional period indirectly helps the couple adjust after the marriage. However, transcultural marriages in the military need more preparation than the Bride's School can provide. In addition, marriage preparatory programs consisting of information and skills essential in marital adjustment such as mutual cultural sharing, cross-cultural communication, creative problem-solving skills, in-law relationships, and effective childrearing practices also are needed by these couples. In addition to experiencing cultural adjustment they will simultaneously experience marital adjustment.

Asian wives struggle to overcome the cultural accommodation phase in intermarriage. They must cope with the cruel external realities of prejudice, limited job opportunity, cultural conflict, and cultural marginality. Many Asian wives tend to display a dual personality and a double consciousness. Their divided loyalty between their own and their husband's cultures induces ambivalence in their attitudes and sentiments. They often feel inferior, excessively self-conscious, and hypersensitive. During the initial phase of cultural transition, social alienation is primarily imposed by the unfamiliar and at times hostile external realities. However, during this second phase of accommodation, psychological alienation becomes more poignant and destructive.

Different social networks are constructed by Asian wives during this phase to ward off social and psychological alienation including bringing their relatives to the United States as a means to incorporate their natal family support system in their new environment. Contrary to initial expectations, interaction with relatives often introduces another spectrum of psychological stress, including value conflicts, competition, jealousy, and financial burden. The relatives may even be reluctant to disclose their association with their Asian-American kin because of bias against transcultural marriage. One interesting study examined the relationship between the racial ethnic group identity of the wife and the family functioning of husbands and wives with the extended family system (Bowen and Henley, 1987). The rejection from extended families may increase the Asian spouse's sense of alienation from her own ethnic group as well as her husband's.

During this accommodation phase, a therapist needs to assist the Asian spouses in utilizing existing mental health and community resources as well as programs specialized in meeting their needs.

The final transculturation phase requires that Asian spouses and their husbands overcome marital tasks as well as normal developmental tasks associated with life-cycle progression. These tasks include effective couple and intrafamilial communication, mutual sharing of personal and cultural strength, functional relationships with various kinship and friendship groups, and effective parenting of biracial or biethnic children.

Marital therapy with transcultural married couples in the military requires additional knowledge, techniques, and skills. In addition to assessing the couple's developmental stage, each spouse's level of personality structure and the level of individuation and extended family and friendship supportive networks, a therapist needs to assess couple dynamics in terms of its revolution and relationship with the military extended family network (Ridenour, 1984). This can affect the service person's physical separation with the spouse and family, branch of military duty, and rank and status. The utilization of the couple's social network system in assessment and problem-solving is needed along with the development of transcultural resources including multilingual and multicultural transculturally married volunteers (Lee, 1982). Lastly, the therapist's knowledge and attitude toward the military, the transcultural marriage, and his/her own ethnicity are important to working with transcultural married couples in the military.

Chapter 7

EXTENDED CASE EXAMPLES

Three cases of intermarried couple therapy are presented. The first case involved an interracial couple with a Caucasian husband and Asian wife. The couple's marital problems centered around conflicts in cultural codes and family life-cycle crisis. Using the ecosystemic framework of transcultural couple therapy, specific techniques and skills employed during various stages of therapy are illustrated along with a cultural transitional map and genogram.

The second case involved an interracial (black husband and Caucasian wife) couple who used negative cultural stereotyping to maximize their racial and cultural differences in child-rearing practices.

Despite the pervasive influence of racial and ethnic factors on intermarried relationships, it is inaccurate to assume that all intermarriage problems stem from racial or ethnic conflicts. The third case presents an interethnic couple (Irish wife and Italian husband) who experienced spouse physical abuse that required immediate attention and intervention. This case demonstrates the importance of crisis intervention, cultural specific assessment and intervention, and utilization of multiple systems in intermarried couple therapy.

Interracial (Caucasian Husband/Asian Wife) Marital Conflicts in Cultural Codes and Family Life-Cycle Crisis

Mrs. I., a forty-five-year-old Filipino/American, was referred to Transcultural Family Institute by her family physician who diagnosed the patient's affective disorder as "psychosomatic" and "neurotic." In addition to periodic depression, Mrs. I. had some minor heart problem. Her depression and family-related problems caused her to occasionally "forget" to take medication for high blood pressure. Mrs. I frequently complained that she had no desire to live any more.

In the initial interview, Mrs. I. impressed me as a small but neatly, well-dressed and well-groomed individual who appeared outwardly friendly and sociable, but inwardly withdrawn and suspicious. Although she seemed to be relieved when she noticed my Asian physical appearance, Mrs. I. avoided direct eye contact with me when I first greeted her. To ease her discomfort and curiosity about my nationality and occupation, I volunteered that I am a naturalized American citizen from Hong Kong and that I help individuals and families with their problems. Mrs. I. responded immediately that she too is a naturalized Asian American from the Philippines. As I nodded my head to establish communication with her, she explained that she had immigrated to the United States twenty years ago with her Anglo/American husband. He had been in the military in the Philippines. Mrs. I. then asked me about my immediate and extended families. I thanked her for her interest. When I told her about my family, I noticed that she began to relax. I then took the opportunity to inquire about her family. Mrs. I. sighed, slumped down, and appeared to be teary. I responded immediately that she must have thought a lot about her family, and that if talking about her family upset her, she could choose to change the topic. Mrs. I. apologized for becoming a "cry-baby" and said "getting emotional has always been my problem." I responded by granting her permission to cry if she felt like it. "Family is a vital part of one's life," I empathized.

Mrs. I. continued that she and her husband have two grown daughters. The older daughter resides in California with her husband and two young children. Her younger daughter, whom Mrs. I. called "baby," married five months earlier. She and her husband moved to a neighboring state after marriage. I complimented her on raising two responsible daughters. Mrs. I. sighed again saying, "It was not easy."

Mrs. I. continued that she missed her daughters very much. As a way to "fill up her lost feeling for her daughters" and to occupy her time, Mrs. I. began baby-sitting in her own home. "I enjoy taking care of babies, but—they are not mine," Mrs. I. said regrettably.

I took the opportunity to assess her relationship with her husband by asking her how her husband had adjusted to their second daughter's departure. Mrs. I shook her head and responded, "It didn't bother him, nothing bothers him." I detected some anger in Mrs. I's voice and I provided her a general lead by commenting, "Your husband reacted differently than you did." Mrs. I. explained that her husband is an "easy-go-lucky" type of person. "He works long hours as a maintenance person for two elementary schools. Between work and after work he drinks with his buddies and visits with his mother who lives in the same town as us," continued Mrs. I. I then asked her how she felt about her husband's activities. Mrs. I. denied by saying angrily, "It doesn't bother me." I clarified by repeating slowly that her husband's long working hours, drinking with his friends, and spending time with his mother did not bother her. Mrs. I. commented, "What is the use!"

"It seems to me that you must have let him know how you felt about this, but that nothing has changed," I empathized.

Mrs. I. then burst into tears saying, "My husband and I have had nothing to do with each other for quite some time. I had my daughters with me then, I was able to cope with it. Now my daughters are gone; I guess I just go crazy." Mrs. I. also volunteered that lately she really did not care about living or dying (which explained why she "forgot" to take her high blood pressure medicine). "If my parents were still alive, I would have packed up and gone back to the Philippines by myself a long time ago," said Mrs. I.

As a means to combat Mrs. I's depression and her low emotional, mental, and physical state, I requested to see her husband as to assess his motivation slowly towards improving marital relationship. Mrs. I. agreed to ask her husband to contact me. Figure 7.1 (end of the case) depicts the couple's cultural transitional map and genogram.

Three days after my first interview with Mrs. I., Mr. I. telephoned me to request a counseling session for him and his wife. I offered him an individual session. Mr. I. rejected and said it was not needed. I interviewed the couple conjointly three days later.

Mr. I. appeared very anxious and eager for the interview to start. He was a physically big, and tall man. He spoke loudly and seemed to intimidate his wife.

After a few sociable exchanges, Mr. I. Commented that he was glad to see an Asian therapist who he believed could help his wife with her problem. I asked Mr. I. how he felt about an Asian therapist, and he replied abruptly, "Okay."

I then asked Mr. I. for his impression of his wife's situation. Mr. I's immediate response was, "It blows my mind." I asked him if he would elaborate on what he meant by "it." Mr. I. said that he did not understand why his wife did not want to do anything, including taking medication to save her life. I inquired if Mr. I understood why his wife did not seem to enjoy living. Mr. I. responded quickly with a low voice and head down. "I wish I knew." To minimize Mr. I's anxiety and potential feelings of threat and guilt, I nurtured him by stating that he must care about his wife since he made an early appointment to see me. Mr. I. spoke with a low but calm voice, "How can you not care about a person you have spent more than twenty years with."

To accentuate the couple's marital bonding, I encouraged them to reminisce about some memorable moments in their marriage. Mrs. I. assumed a less active verbal part in reminiscing, but she smiled and nodded to show her approval of her husband's stories about their relationship. To focus on the presenting problem, I asked about the couple's present relationship. Mr. I. responded defensively, "What relationship?" I empathized by stating how much both of them were hurting.

I acknowledged Mr. I's hurt, and I challenged him to gain an understanding of his wife's present predicament and social isolation. "I understand," whispered Mr. I. with his head down again, "but I do not know what to do."

I turned to Mrs. I. for suggestions. After a long pause, Mrs. I. admitted that she had not been "much of a wife" to her husband. She then complained that she and her husband had nothing in common. They had different interests, and they never saw things the same. Because Mr. I. was a protestant, she had ceased to attend Catholic church much earlier. "Since I don't go to Catholic church, I have no contact at all with my close Filipino friends who are Catholics," complained Mrs. I. "Just because I do not think the way you do and do not do the same things you and your American friends do does not mean that my way is wrong. I hate it when you use stereotypes to put me down simply because of my Asian ancestry," continued Mrs. I. Mr. I. sat up straight—and appeared to be startled, "strange enough, this is exactly how I feel too. You think your Asian way is superior to the American way. I cannot stand it when you call me a big-mouthed American."

I explained to the couple the dynamics and inherent cultural value conflicts intermarried couples usually experience. In addition, I shared with them the potential richness in mutual sharing between interracial couples (Ho, 1984) who experience cultural transition. Instead of widening the cultural gap and value differences, I challenged the couple to find commonalities that could repair and solidify their marital bondage. Mrs. I. responded by saying, "Since we have never established a solid marital bond, I really do not know where and how to repair it." Mr. I. appeared to be offended by Mrs. I's statement and he stated that as far as he was concerned, they got along fine when they were first married. Mrs. I. responded that during the initial period of their marriage, they tried their best to minimize their differences. "Besides, I didn't want my parents and relatives to think that I made a mistake by marrying an American instead of a Filipino," added Mrs. I. Before the session ended,

I encouraged the couple to recapitulate the parts of our discussion that had special meaning for them. Both partners agreed that although they felt uncomfortable and apprehensive, they were pleased to have an opportunity to ventilate their feelings. Mrs. I. expressed surprise to learn about her husband's emotional hurt and feelings of isolation. Mr. I. indicated that this was the longest and most helpful talk they had had with each other for quite some time. He also expressed hope that his relationship with his wife would improve, and that his wife's depression would be lifted. The couple agreed to return for four more sessions aiming to improve their marital relationship.

The next three sessions with this couple were devoted to engaging them in communicating effectively with each other. Essential communication styles and skills for conflict resolution were taught. Assignments were given so the couple could practice these skills at home. Despite the couple's strong motivation to learn about new communication skills, occasionally their interaction ran into barricades. The couple's old hurt and resentment erupted when they focused on personal personality deficits instead of cultural differences. The couple's newly learned problem-solving skills gradually helped them to disagree agreeably. As a result, they began to enjoy spending time together at home. Mr. I. also encouraged his wife to rejoin the Catholic church to resume her fellowship with several Filipino families and interracial families. As the couple began to reconcile and find companionship with each other, Mr. I. drastically reduced the time he spent with his friends. Mr. I's mother was somewhat puzzled and upset with her son's infrequent visits, but she later learned to accept her daughter-in-law as a means to entice her son to visit her. Two months after the last counseling session, Mrs. I. paid me a surprise visit. She brought me freshly cooked banana dumplings. She informed me that she felt much better, and her physician had decided that she no longer needed medication for high blood pressure.

Interracial (Black Husband/Caucasian Wife) Marital Conflict in Childrearing Practice

The next case example involves an interracial marriage between Mr. Fairchild, a thirty-two-year-old Black, and his thirty-year-old Caucasian wife. The couple's daughter, Jennifer, aged nine, had displayed problem behavior involving incessant pulling and twirling of her hair, baby talking, and throwing severe temper tantrums. The school counselor

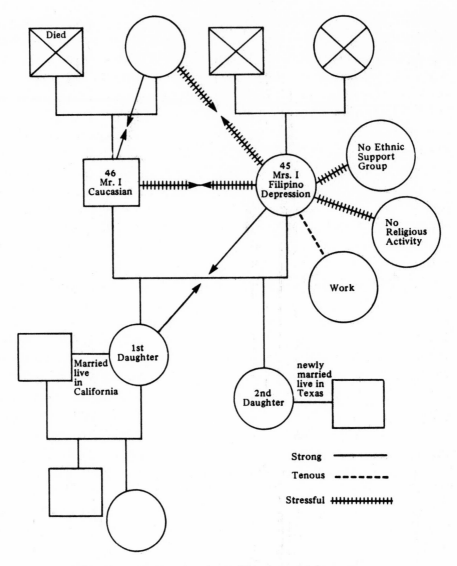

Figure 7.1. Couple's cultural transitional map and genogram.

concluded that Jennifer's problem was related to her home environment.
Jennifer's parents were requested to come for counseling, but Jennifer's
father repeatedly refused to comply using "inability to get off from work"
as the reason. When the school reported it might no longer be able to
keep Jennifer because of her behavior, the couple agreed to see a therapist of their choice.

I suggested I first see the family together as a unit. Mr. Fairchild was
half an hour late for the interview. As soon as he sat down, he glanced at
his wife and said, "I guess my wife has told you everything you need to

know." I responded that I was glad that he could come and that his presence would be a great help to me in assisting his daughter in school. Mr. Fairchild said that Jennifer's problem was caused mainly by a racist school, counselors, and teachers. "If Jennifer looked more like her mother than me, she would be all right," he declared. I empathized by listing some disadvantages minority students face in a predominately white school. Mrs. Fairchild interrupted by saying, "My husband and I do not agree with each other on disciplining Jennifer." As the parents defended their respective positions regarding disciplining their daughter, I asked Jennifer how she felt about her parents' exchange. Jennifer responded that she was glad that she was not the "troubled one" this time and that she wished her parents could get along better. To protect Mr. Fairchild from overdisclosure of his personal feelings before trust was established with me as the counselor, I invited him to return for the next session by himself. I also told Mrs. Fairchild that I would like to interview her privately in the near future.

Mr. Fairchild commented in the next session that it was not easy for him to discuss feelings, especially with whites. "You'll get into a lot of trouble in this world if you let the white folks know too much about you," he declared. I remarked, "Your wife is white." "This might be the problem, exactly," he responded. Apologetically, he explained that in some ways, his wife was different from the ordinary white. "She pursued me when both of us were in college; that angered all the white boys," Mr. Fairchild bragged. He then explained that he and his wife got along well after marriage until they moved to this community where her parents resided. "I cannot stand her family, especially her father; that old man never accepted me," complained Mr. Fairchild. "When he tells me what to do, including how to handle Jennifer, I say to myself, 'that's it, that's all I can take.' "

I asked Mr. Fairchild about his wife's reaction to his relationship with her father. He replied, "She doesn't care how I feel; she is always busy defending her father's position. She's lazy, just sitting at home doing nothing except spoiling Jennifer," complained Mr. Fairchild. In an attempt to assist him in understanding the racial and cultural differences between him and his wife, I encouraged him to tell me about his own home background. He spoke with pride of his hard-working mother and boasted that she had tried very hard not to spoil him as he was growing up. Her persistent efforts to bring up Jennifer as a "tough cookie" had contributed most to the disagreement between him and his wife.

To assist Mr. Fairchild in understanding the dilemma Jennifer was facing, I asked him how he would feel if he was Jennifer. Mr. Fairchild agreed that he knew Jennifer was put in a bind. "I'm ashamed that sometimes I use Jennifer to get back at and even with my wife," said Mr. Fairchild. "I guess my wife and I better get our act together," suggested Mr. Fairchild. I agreed.

My interview with Mrs. Fairchild revealed basically the same family dynamics but from her cultural viewpoint. Mrs. Fairchild's southern background had taught her that the mother's place was at home, especially when her child was young. She resented her husband's comparing her with his mother. His reluctance to express his true, deep feelings had driven her "against the wall." Mrs. Fairchild recognized the need to improve her relationship with her husband as a necessary step in resolving their daughter's adjustment problems at school.

The next three therapy sessions centered on means to improve understanding and communication between the couple. I encouraged them to deemphasize the black and white cultural factors in their relationship. Instead, improved ways to understand and appreciate each other without stereotyped projections and interpretations were stressed. In disciplining Jennifer, they were encouraged to place emphasis on simplicity, concreteness, and practicality. They were to focus on their daughter's real needs rather than on philosophical and cultural orientations.

Mr. Fairchild's hostility toward his father-in-law was lessened when Mrs. Fairchild said she no longer felt the need to defend her father. Although mutual acceptance between Mr. Fairchild and his father-in-law would not occur immediately and might never be realized, nevertheless, Mr. Fairchild came to understand that they did not have to treat each other as enemies. He realized that their continued animosity could jeopardize the Fairchild marriage. The couple's counseling with me was interrupted when the family moved out of town. Mrs. Fairchild wrote me a month after their move to tell me that her relationship with her husband had improved and that Jennifer so far had been adjusting well in their new home and at school. Mrs. Fairchild had resented the family's relocation initially, but related that she could now see the value of not living close to her parents.

Interethnic (Irish Wife/Italian Husband) Spouse Physical Abuse

Sharon, an Irish-American woman, aged 33, has been physically abused ever since she married her Italian-American husband, Tony three years ago. Sharon has been in and out of the police station, hospital emergency ward, and the battered women's shelter for help. Occasionally, she managed to stay with her friends a few days when her husband's abusive behavior became intolerable. Despite her friends', hospital workers', and shelter counselor's persistent advice and requests to leave her husband, Sharon eventually returned to Tony, after he apologized to her. The last physical abuse Sharon received was so severe that it became life-threatening. Sharon claimed that the abuse was severe simply because she decided not to leave home, because she felt she had run out places to hide from her problems. She believed that her friends and helping professionals had grown unsympathetic and impatient with her. Besides, she was tired of listening to the professionals implying that both she and her husband were mentally ill and needed psychiatric treatment. Sharon denied, by insisting that her husband was a fine and loving person who just occasionally lost his temper when he felt jealous or when Sharon was indifferent to him. Sharon insisted that she loved her husband and marriage.

The therapist was empathic to Sharon's situation and he was supportive of Sharon's commitment to her husband. If she decided to try this new idea of convincing her husband at all costs, she should do it when her husband was calm and before the violence erupted.

The very next day after the interview, Sharon telephoned the therapist to explain her new strategy of providing her husband with a baseball bat as a means to convince him of her true love and devotion to him. Sharon reported that her husband first did not know what to make of her proposal. After a few uneasy chuckles, her husband broke into tears. He embraced her and repeatedly told Sharon that he loved her and could not hurt her again.

Sharon was elated. The therapist capitalized on her positive experience by informing her that he would like to see the couple for consultation regarding their future relationship. Sharon commented that after the "touching incident" which had resulted in both embracing each other to insure their love, her husband had expressed interest in thanking the therapist personally. However, Sharon said that her husband did not feel comfortable coming to the office, but the couple would like to invite the therapist to their home for dinner.

The therapist accepted the invitation. The couple saw the therapist six more times, first three times at their own home and the last three times at the therapist's office. The husband's vow not to hurt Sharon coupled with their newly acquired skills in couple communication improved the relationship. There was no abuse incidence reported during the next two-month period after therapy had terminated.

This case example demonstrates several important issues in the treatment of an intermarried couple who are experiencing a life-threatening situation and who are highly resistant to change strategy traditionally employed by therapists. The professionals' advice to the wife seemed logical and reasonable, but it did not represent the wife's view of the problem and how the problem should be resolved. Most importantly, the professionals did not realize the commitment and seriousness of the wife's decision to stay in the marriage, consistent with the Irish Catholic belief that marriage is for life.

Because of the serious life-threatening physical violence, the therapist elected to deal with the couple's interactional crisis first, the ethnicity issue second, the couple's and the husband's personality third, and the couple's communication and relationship last.

At the onset of the therapy, the wife would have dismissed therapy if the therapist had emphasized the couple's ethnicity or personality dynamic especially as related to the wife's refusal to leave her husband after repeated abusive incidents. On the other hand, the husband's historic violent abusive behavior would not cease if the couple's relationship issues were not dealt with and resolved. Resolving the couple's relationship issues required understanding each spouse's ethnicity as it related to the formation and continuation of the marital relationship, especially in the area of conflict resolution. The husband's emotional and expressive temperament, characteristic of Italian men, was put to a severe test by his passive-aggressive Irish wife who employed unemotional responses and silence to express her noncompliance. Therapy with this couple had to center around validation of each spouse's behavioral traits and then expand their old patterns of interaction conducive to nonviolence and a harmonious relationship.

Appendix A

INTERMARRIAGE POTENTIALS INVENTORY (IPI)

Intermarriage Potentials Inventory (IPI) is a tool designed to aid individuals who:

(1) prepare couples for intermarriage
(2) counsel couples experiencing intermarital problems
(3) counsel couples for intermarriage enrichment

Specifically, the inventory identifies eight important issues encountered by engaged and intermarried couples. These issues include: (1) realistic expectations, (2) role expectations, (3) cultural orientation, (4) financial management, (5) sexual relationship, (6) children and marriage, (7) communication, and (8) conflict resolution.

An important goal in developing the IPI was to have an instrument that would be relatively easy to administer and score. While at the same time it would enhance the therapist's ability to "help couples help themselves." Therapists using this instrument should be reminded that IPI is only one of many tools that can be used to help a couple assess their own readiness for marriage or identify areas of their relationship that need strengthening. This is a relatively easy inventory to score, but its full potential depends upon the respondent's willingness to answer the statements completely and honestly.

Intermarriage Potentials Inventory

Instructions to individual who wishes to take this inventory:

The Intermarriage Potentials Inventory is not a test. There are no right or wrong answers. It is designed to help you learn more about your **relationship** with your partner.

Please respond to all statements according to your point of view. The maximum usefulness of this statement depends upon your **willingness** to respond **fully** and **honestly**.

Instructions: Answer **every** question. Circle one number for each statement.

Following are some statements made by engaged or intermarried individuals. How often do you feel this way in your relationship with your partner?

In my relationship with my partner, I . . .	Always	Fre-quently	Occa-sionally	Seldom	Never
A. Do not expect him/her to meet all my needs.	5	4	3	2	1
B. Believe in sharing household and other responsibilities.	5	4	3	2	1

117

In my relationship with my partner, I . . .	Always	Fre-quently	Occa-sionally	Seldom	Never
C. Show respect for his/her culture.	5	4	3	2	1
D. Desire a general plan for how much money we can spend each month.	5	4	3	2	1
E. Find it easy and comfortable to talk with him/her about sexual issues.	5	4	3	2	1
F. Am satisfied with our discussions regarding the values and goals that we want for our children.	5	4	3	2	1
G. Find it easy to express all my true feelings to him/her.	5	4	3	2	1
H. Do not hesitate to bring up con-flicting views in discussion.	5	4	3	2	1
I. Consider our relationship the number one priority in my search for happiness in life.	5	4	3	2	1
J. Believe in shared decision making.	5	4	3	2	1
K. Want to search out and share cultural beliefs with him/her.	5	4	3	2	1
L. Am happy with our management of financial matters.	5	4	3	2	1
M. Am satisfied with our decisions regarding family planning.	5	4	3	2	1
N. Am satisfied with our discussions about how our children should be raised and our role as father/mother.	5	4	3	2	1
O. Am satisfied with how (skill) he/she and I talk with each other.	5	4	3	2	1
P. Am committed to resolving issues that concern both of us.	5	4	3	2	1
Q. Believe in working hard constantly to maintain a high (productive) level of interaction	5	4	3	2	1

In my relationship with my partner, I ...	Always	Fre-quently	Occa-sionally	Seldom	Never
R. Am not hung up with traditional roles and responsibilities.	5	4	3	2	1
S. Believe in the need for active involvement and cultural integration.	5	4	3	2	1
T. Am satisfied with our decisions about how much money we should save.	5	4	3	2	1
U. Am satisfied with the amount of affection (physical/emotional) he/she shows me.	5	4	3	2	1
V. Am satisfied with our interaction with our extended family and their relationships with each of us.	5	4	3	2	1
W. Am not hesitant to let him/her know what I want.	5	4	3	2	1
X. Am satisfied with my skills (listening to partner, expressing feelings and wants, etc.) in problem solving concerning both of us.	5	4	3	2	1

Instructions for scoring follow:

1. Enter the number you have circled for each question in the spaces below, putting the number you have circled to Question A over line A, to Question B over line B, etc.
2. Add the 3 scores on each line to get your totals. For example, the sum of your scores over lines A, I and Q gives you your score on **Realistic Expectations.**

Relationship Categories

___ + ___ + ___ = _____
 A   I   Q   Realistic Expectations

___ + ___ + ___ = _____
 B   J   R   Role Expectations

___ + ___ + ___ = _____
 C   K   S   Cultural Orientation

___ + ___ + ___ = _____
 D   L   T   Financial Management

___ + ___ + ___ = _____
 E   M   U   Sexual Relationship

Relationship Categories

___ + ___ + ___	=	_____		
F N V		Children and Extended Family		
___ + ___ + ___	=	_____		
G O W		Communication		
___ + ___ + ___	=	_____		
H P X		Conflict Resolution		

Scores can vary from 3 to 15 for each category. Any score 11 and above is high; 7 and below is low. Your scores reflect the strengths and potential problems in your relationship.

Appendix B

ETHNIC-COMPETENCE-INVENTORY (ECI)

Here are some statements made by marital therapists with intermarried couples. How often do you feel this way when you work with intermarried couples?

Circle one number of each question
ANSWER EVERY QUESTION.

In work with intermarried couples, I ...	Always	Fre-quently	Occa-sionally	Seldom	Never
A. Realize the couple's ethnic minority reality, including the effects of racism and poverty on the couple.	5	4	3	2	1
B. Am able to understand and "tune in" to the couple's cultural dispositions, behaviors, and structure which may include close extended family ties.	5	4	3	2	1
C. Am able to utilize cultural mapping to ascertain the couple problem.	5	4	3	2	1
D. Clearly delineate agency functions and respectfully inform the family of my professional expectations of them.	5	4	3	2	1
E. Am able to reaffirm the couple's life skills and coping strategies within a bicultural environment.	5	4	3	2	1
F. Am able to assess the accomplish- of therapeutic goals according to the couple's individualist/collectivist culture.	5	4	3	2	1
G. Understand the couple's ethnicity, language, social class and differences in minority status, such as refugees, immigrants, or native born.	5	4	3	2	1

In work with intermarried couples, I . . .	Always	Fre-quently	Occa-sionally	Seldom	Never
H. Am able to discuss openly racial and ethnic differences and issues and respond to culturally based cues.	5	4	3	2	1
I. Am aware of the ecosystemic sources (racism, poverty and prejudice) of many couple problems.	5	4	3	2	1
J. Am able to formulate goals consistent with the couple's emphasis on familism and interdependence.	5	4	3	2	1
K. Am able to "frame" the change within the traditional, culturally acceptable language	5	4	3	2	1
L. Am able to reconnect and restore the couple to their larger world or environment.	5	4	3	2	1
M. Am aware of my own culture/ ethnicity and professional culture (marriage and family, social work, psychology, etc.) which may be different than the couple's own culture and ethnicity.	5	4	3	2	1
N. Am able to adapt to the couple's interactive style and language, conveying to the couple that I understand, value, and validate their life strategies.	5	4	3	2	1
O. Can identify the links between ecosystemic problems, couple interactive problems, and individual concerns or problems.	5	4	3	2	1
P. Am able to differentiate and select from three categories of goals: situational stress (e.g., social isolation, poverty), cultural transition (e.g., conflictual rearing practice), and transcultural dysfunctional patterns (e.g., developmental impasses and repetitive interactional behaviors).	5	4	3	2	1

In work with intermarried couples, I . . .	Always	Frequently	Occasionally	Seldom	Never
Q. Am able to suggest a change or new strategy as an expansion of the "old" cultural stress or problem-solving response.	5	4	3	2	1
R. Am able to assist the couple to incorporate the new changes in the couple's original life strategy independent of the therapist's interaction.	5	4	3	2	1
S. Am sensitive to the couple's fear of racist or prejudiced orientations.	5	4	3	2	1
T. Am able to understand the couple's help-seeking behavior which includes the couple's conceptualization of the problem and the manner by which the problem can be solved.	5	4	3	2	1
U. Consider the implications of what is being suggested in relation to each couple's cultural reality (unique dispositions, life strategies, and experiences).	5	4	3	2	1
V. Am able to engage the couple to formulate a goal that is problem-focused, structured, realistic, concrete, practical, and readily achievable.	5	4	3	2	1
W. Am aware that application of change strategies is consistent with the couple's need and problem, degree of acculturation, motivation for change, and comfort in responding to the therapist's directives.	5	4	3	2	1
X. Consider the ethnic minority couple's concept of time and space in a relationship during termination and make sure the termination is natural and gradual.	5	4	3	2	1

How to Score

1. Enter the number you have circled for each question in the space below, putting the number you have circled to Question A over line A, to Question B over line B, etc.

2. Add the 4 scores on each line to get your totals. For example, the sum of your scores over lines A, G, M, and S gives you your score on skills during Precontact phase; line B, H, N, and T give the score on Problem Identification, etc.

Total

___ + ___ + ___ + ___ = _____
A   G   M   S   Pre-Contact

___ + ___ + ___ + ___ = _____
B   H   N   T   Problem-Identification

___ + ___ + ___ + ___ =
C   I   O   U   Problem-Specification

___ + ___ + ___ + ___ = _____
D   J   P   V   Mutual-Goal-Formulation

___ + ___ + ___ + ___ = _____
E   K   Q   W   Problem-Solving

___ + ___ + ___ + ___ = _____
F   L   R   X   Termination

BIBLIOGRAPHY

Ackerman, N.: The Psychodynamic of Family Life. New York: Basic Books, 1961.

Acosta, F.: Ethnic Variables in Psychotherapy: The Mexican American. In G. Martinez (Ed.): Chicano Psychology. New York: Academic Press, 1977.

Acosta, F. et al.: Effective Psychotherapy for Low-Income and Minority Patients. New York: Plenum Press, 1982.

Alvirez, D. et al.: The Mexican American Family. In C. Mindel and R. Habenstein (Eds.): Ethnic Families in America. New York: Elsevier, 1981.

Aponte, H: Family Therapy and the Community. In M. Gibbs (Ed.): Community Psychology. New York: Gardner Press, 1979.

Aunda, D.: Bicultural Socialization: Factors Affecting the Minority Experience. Social Work, 29:101–107, 1984.

Banks, W.: The Differential Effects of Race and Social Class on Helping. Journal of Clinical Psychology, 28: 90–92, 1972.

Barrera, M. Mexican American Mental Health Service Utilization: A Critical Examination of Some Proposed Variables. Community Mental Health Journal, 14:35–45, 1978.

Bell, R.: The Relative Importance of Mother and Wife Rules Among Lower Class Women. In R. Staples (Ed.): The Black Family, Essays and Studies. Belmont, CA: Wadsworth, 1971.

Bellah, R. et al.: Habits of the Heart: Individualism and Commitment in American Life. Berkeley: University of California Press, 1985.

Benson, S.: Ambiguous Ethnicity. London: Cambridge University Press. 1981.

Bowen, M. Family Therapy in Clinical Practice. New York: Jason Aronson, 1978.

Bowen, G. and Henley, C.: Asian-Wife Marriages in the U.S. Military. Family Perspective, 21: 23–37, 1987.

Bride's School in Korea. Military Family, 2: 5, 1982.

Brislin, R.: Crosscultural Encounters. New York: Pergamon, 1981.

Brown, E. and Shaughnessy, T.: Education for Social Work Practice with American Indian Families. Washington, D.C.: U.S. Department of Health and Human Services, 1982.

Bryden, J.: An Acoustic and Social Dialect Analysis. Charlottesville, VA: University of Virginia, 1968.

Burden, D.: Single Parents and the Work Setting: The Impact of Multiple Job and Homelife Responsibilities. Family Relations, 35: 37–43, 1986.

Casas, S. and Keefe, S.: Family and Mental Health in Mexican American Community. Los Angeles, CA: Spanish Speaking Mental Health Research Center, 1978.

Cerroni-Long, E.: Marrying Out: Socio-Cultural and Psychological Implications of Intermarriage. Journal of Comparative Family Studies, 16: 25–46, 1985.

Char, W.: Motivations for Intercultural Marriages. In W. Tseng et al. (Ed.): Adjustment in Intercultural Marriage. Honolulu, HI: University Press of Hawaii, 1977.

Collins, G.: International Children Are More Successful than Myths Suggest. Oakland Tribune. Oakland, CA, June 26, p. 1, 1984.

Cortese, M.: Intervention Research with Hispanic Americans: A Review. Hispanic Journal of Behavioral Sciences, 1:4–20, 1979.

Crester, G. and Leon, J. (Eds.): Intermarriage in the United States. New York: Haworth Press, 1982.

DeGeyndi, W.: Health Behavior and Health Needs in Urban Indians in Minneapolis. Health Service Reports, 88: 360–366, 1973.

D.I.A.N.D.: The Canadian Indian: Statistics. Ottawa: Indian Affairs, 1975.

Doherty, W. and Colangelo, N.: The Family FIRO Model: A Modest Proposal for Organizing Family Treatment. Journal of Marriage and Family Therapy, 10:19–29, 1984.

Duberman, L.: The Reconstituted Family: A Study of Remarried Couples and Their Children. Chicago: Nelson-Hall, 1975.

Falicov, C.: Mexican Americans. In M. McGoldrick et al. (Eds.): Ethnicity and Family Therapy. New York: Guilford, 1982.

Falicov, C. and Brudner-White, L.: The Shifting Family Triangle: The Issue of Cultural and Contextual Relativity. In C. Falicov (Ed.): Cultural Perspectives in Family Therapy. Rockville, MD: Aspen Systems, 1983.

Feldman, L.: Integrative Multi-Level Therapy: A Comprehensive Interpersonal and Intrapsychic Approach. Journal of Marriage and Family Therapy, 11: 357–372, 1986.

Fine, M., Schwebel, A., and Myers, L.: The Effects of World View on Adaptation of Single Parenthood Among Adult Middle-Class Women. Journal of Family Issues, 6:107–127, 1985.

Finkelstein, L.: Toward an Object-Relations Approach in Psychoanalytic Marital Therapy. Journal of Marital and Family Therapy, 13: 287–298, 1987.

Friedman, E.: Systems and Ceremonies: A Family's View of Rites of Passage. In E. Carter and M. McGoldrick (Eds.): The Family Life Cycle, A Framework for Family Therapy. New York: Gardner, 1980.

Fujii, S.: Elderly Asian Americans and Use of Public Service. Social Casework, 57: 202–207, 1976.

Geland, D. and Kutzik, A. Ethnicity and Aging. New York, Springer, 1979.

Giordano, J.: The Ethno-Cultural Factor in Mental Health: A Literature Review and Bibliography. New York: Institute on Pluralism and Group Identity, 1977.

Glasser, I.: Guidelines for Using an Interpreter in Social work. Child Welfare, 62: 468–470, 1983.

Golden, J.: Facilitating Factors in Negro-White Intermarriage. Phylon, 20: 273–284, 1959.

Gordon, A.: Intermarriage: Interfaith, Interracial, Interethnic. Westport, CT: Greenwood Press, 1980.

Gordon, W.: Basic Constructs for an Integrative and Generative Conception of Social Work. In G. Hearn (Ed.): Council on Social Work Education, 1969.

Greenberg, L. and Johnson, S.: Emotionally Focused Couples Therapy: An Integrated Affective Systematic Approach. In N. Jacobson and A. Gurman (Eds.): The Clinical Handbook of Marital Therapy. New York: Guilford Press, 1986.

Griffith, M.: The Influences of Race on the Psychotherapeutic Relationship. Psychiatry, 40:27–40, 1977.

Halem, L.: Separated and Divorced Women. Westport, CT: Greenwood Press, 1982.

Haley, J.: Problem-Solving Therapy: New Strategies for Effective Family Therapy. San Francisco: Jossey-Bass, 1976.

Hanson, W.: The Urban Indian Woman and Her Family. Social Casework, 61: 476–484, 1980.

Hartman, A.: Finding Families: An Ecological Approach to Family Assessment in Adoption. Newbury Park, CA: Sage, 1979.

Heer, D.: Intermarriage. In S. Thernstrom et al. (Eds.): Harvard Encyclopedia of American Ethnic Groups. Cambridge, Mass.: Harvard University Press, 1980.

Hippler, A.: The North Alaska Eskimos: A Culture and Personality Perspective. American Ethnologist, 1: 449–469, 1974.

Ho, M.: and McDowell, E.: The Black Worker-White Client Relationship. Clinical Social Work Journal, 1: 161–167, 1973.

Ho, M.: Building a Successful Intermarriage. St. Meinrad, IN: 1984.

Ho, M.: Family Therapy with Ethnic Minorities. Newbury Park, CA: Sage, 1987.

Ho, M.: Applying Family Therapy Theories to Asian/Pacific Americans. Contemporary Family Therapy, 11: 61–70, 1989.

Holmes, T. and Masada, M.: Life Change and Illness Susceptibility. In B. Dohrenwend and P. Dohrenwend (Eds.): Stressful Life Events: Their Nature and Effects. New York: John Wiley, 1974.

Hetherington, E.: Children and Divorce. In R. Henderson (Ed.): Parent-child Interaction: Theory, Research and Prospect. New York: Academic Press, 1981.

Hotstede, G.: Cultures Consequences: Beverly Hills, CA: Sage, 1980.

Hsu, F.: American Museum Science Book. Garden City, NY: Doubleday, 1972.

Hynes, K. and Werbin, J.: Group Psychotherapy for Spanish-speaking Women, Psychiatric Annals, 7, 52–63, 1977.

Inkeles, A.: The American Character. The Center Magazine, 25–39, 1983.

Jacobson, N. and Margolin, G.: Marital Therapy. New York: Brunner/Mazel, 1979.

Jester, K. Analytic Essay: Intercultural and Intermarriage. In G. Crester and J. Leon (Eds): Intermarriage in the United States. New York: Haworth Press, 1982.

Jones, D.: The Urban Native Encounters the Social Service System. Fairbanks: University of Alaska, 1974.

Jones, D.: The Mystique of Expertise in the Social Service. Journal of Sociology and Social Welfare, 3: 332–346, 1977.

Jones, E.: Effects of Race on Psychotherapy Process and Outcome: An Exploratory Investigation. Psychotherapy: Theory, Research and Practice, 15:226–236, 1984.

Keith, D. and Whitaker, C.: C'est La Guerre: Military Families and Family Therapy. In F. Kaslow and R. Ridenour (Eds.): The Military Family. New York: Guilford Press, 1984.

Kernberg, O.: Object-Relations Theory and Clinical Psychoanalysis. New York: Jason Aronson, 1976.

Kich, G.: Eurasians: Ethnic/Racial Identity Development of Biracial Japanese/White Adults. Unpublished Doctoral Dissertation, Wright Institute: Berkeley, CA, 1982.

Kim, B.: Asian Wives of U.S. Servicemen: Women in Shadows. Amerasia Journal, 4: 91–145, 1981.

Kitano, H. and Yeung, W.: Chinese Interracial Marriage. In G. Crester and J. Leon (Eds.): Intermarriage in the United States. New York: Haworth Press, 1982.

Kohut, H.: Thoughts on Narcissism and Narcissistic Rage. Psychoanalytic Study of the Child, 27: 360–400, 1972.

Kohut, H.: How Does Analysis Cure? Chicago: University of Chicago Press, 1984.

Kleinman, A. and Lin, T.: Normal and Deviant Behavior in Chinese Culture. Hingham, MA: Reidel, 1981.

Ladefoged, P. and Broadbent, D.: Information Conveyed by Vowels. Journal of the Acoustical Society of America, 29:98–104, 1957.

Lapug, L.: A Study of Psychopathology. Queszon City: University of the Philippines Press, 1973.

Lee, D.: Asian-Born Spouses: Stresses and Coping Patterns. Military Family, 2: 3–5, 1982.

Lerande, D.: Family Theories as a Necessary Component of Family Therapy. Social Casework, 57:271–295, 1976.

Lewis, J. et al.: No Single Thread: Psychological Health in Family Systems. New York: Brunner and Mazel, 1976.

Leslie, G.: The Family in Social Context. New York: Oxford University Press, 1982.

Lyles, M. et al.: Racial Identity and Self Esteem. Journal of American Academy of Child Psychiatry. 24: 150–153, 1985.

Madanes, C.: Behind the One-Way Mirror. San Francisco. Jossey-Bass, 1984.

McAdoo, H.: Family Therapy in the Black Community. Journal of the American Orthopsychiatric Association, 47:74–79, 1977.

Martin, E. and Martin, J.: The Black Extended Family. Chicago: University of Chicago Press, 1978.

Mass, A.: Asian as Individuals: The Japanese Community. Social Casework, 57: 160–164, 1976.

McGoldrick, M. et al. (Eds.): Ethnicity and Family Therapy. New York: Guilford, 1982.

McGoldrick, M. and Preto, N.: Ethnic Intermarriage: Implications for Therapy. Family Process, 23: 347–364, 1984.

McGoldrick, M. and Rohrbaugh, M.: Researching Ethnic Family Stereotypes, Family Process, 26:89–99, 1987.

Miller, S. Nunally, E. and Wackman, D. Alive and Aware. Minneapolis: Interpersonal Communication Program, 1975.

Minuchin, S.: Structural Family Therapy. Cambridge: Harvard University Press, 1974.

Monahan, T.: Are Interracial Marriages Really Less Stable? Social Forces, 48:461–473, 1970.

Mullings, L.: Anthropological Perspectives on Afro-American Family. In M. Thompson-Fullilove (Ed.): The Black Family: Mental Health Perspectives. Proceeding of Second Annual Black Task Force, 1985.

Norlin, J. and Ho, M.: Co-Worker Approach to Working with Families. Clinical Social work, 2: 127–124, 1974.

Orthner, D. and Bowen, G.: Families in Blue: Insights from Air Force families in the Pacific. Greensboro, NC: Family Development Press, 1982.

Padilla, A.: Pluralistic Counseling and Psychotherapy for Hispanic Americans. In A. Marsella (Ed.): Cross-Cultural Counseling and Psychotherapy. New York: Pergamon, 1981.

Padilla, A., Carlos, M., and Keefe, S.: Mental Health Service Utilization by Mexican American. In M. Miranda (Ed.): Psychotherapy with the Spanish-Speaking: Issues in Research and Service Delivery. Los Angeles: Spanish Speaking Mental Health Research Center, University of California, 1976.

Pendagast, S. and Sherman, R.: Diagrammatic Assessment of Family Relationship. Social Casework, 59: 465–476, 1977.

Pilisuk, E. and Parks, T.: A Framework and Themes for Social Network Intervention. Family Process, 23: 187–204, 1984.

Pollak, O.: The Broken Family. In N. Cohen (Ed.): Social Work and Social Problems. New York: National Association of Social Workers, 1964.

Porterfield, E.: Black and White Mixed Marriages: An Ethnographic Study of Black-White Families. Chicago: Nelson Hall, 1978.

Rankin, R. and Maneker, J.: Correlates of Marital Duration and Black-White Intermarriage in California. In C. Everett (Ed.): Minority and Ethnic Issues in the Divorce Process. New York: Haworth, 1988.

Reiss, D.: The Family Construction of Reality. Cambridge, MA: Harvard University Press, 1981.

Reiss, I.: Family Systems in America. Hinsdale, IL: Dryden Press, 1976.

Ridenour, R.: The Military, Service Families, and the Therapist. In F. Kaslow and R. Ridenour (Eds.): The Military Family. New York: Guilford Press, 1984.

Robbins, G. and Tooney, J.: Innovative Use of the FIRO–B in Couple Counseling. Journal of Marriage and Family Counseling. 2:277–282, 1976.

Rodgers-Rose, L.: The Black Women. Beverly Hills, CA: Sage, 1980.

Rodriquez, A.: Special Treatment Needs of Children of Military Families. In F. Kaslow and R. Ridenour (Eds.): The Military Family. New York: Guilford Press, 1984.

Rounsaville, B. and Chevron, E.: Interpersonal Psych. Therapy: Clinical Application. In A. Rush (Ed).: Short-term Psychotherapies for Depression. New York: Guilford, 1982.

Rozensky, R. and Gomez, M.: Language Switching in Psychotherapy with Bilinguals: Two Problems, two models, and Case Examples. Psychotherapy: Theory, Research and Practice, 20: 152–160, 1983.

Satir, V.: Conjoint Family Therapy—Palo Alto, CA: Science and Behavior Books, 1967.

Schwabe, M. and Kaslow, F.: Violence in the Military Family. In F. Kaslow and R. Ridenour (Eds.) The Military Family. New York: Guilford Press, 1984.

Schutz, W.: FIRO: A Three Dimensional Theory of Interpersonal Behavior. New York: Holt, Rinehart, 1958.

Seelye, H. and Wasilewski, J.: Toward a Taxonomy of Coping Strategies Used in Multicultural Settings. Paper presented at the meeting of the Society for Intercultural Education, Training and Research, Mexico City, 1979.

Shimkin, D. et al.: The Extended Black Family in Black Societies. The Hague: Mouton Publishers, 1978.

Sluzki, C.: Migration and Family Conflict. Family Process, 18: 379–39, 1979.

Solomon, B.: Black Empowerment: Social Work in Oppressed Communities. New York: Columbia University Press, 1976.

Spiegel, J.: Transactions Inquiry: Description of Systems. In J. Papajohn (Ed.): Transactions: The Interplay Between Individual Family and Society. New York: Science House, 1971.

Stevens, E.: Marianismo: The Other Face at Machismo. In A. Pecastello (Ed.): Female and Male in Latin America. Pittsburgh: University of Pittsburg Press, 1973.

Stinnett, N. and DeFrain, J.: The Secrets of Strong Families. Boston, MA: Little Brown, 1986.

Stuart, I. and Abt, L. (Eds.): Interracial Marriage: Expectations and Realities. New York: Grossman Publishers, 1973.

Stuart, R.: Helping Couple Change: A Social Learning Approach to Marital Therapy. New York: Guilford, 1980.

Stack, C.: All Our Kin. New York: Harper and Row, 1974.

Sue, D.: Counseling the Culturally Different: Theory and Practice. New York: Wiley, 1981.

Teicher, J.: Some Observations on Identity Problems in Children of Negro-White Marriages. Journal of Nervous and Mental Disease, 146: 249–256, 1968.

Theorensen, C. and Mahoney, M.: Behavioral Self-Control. New York: Holt, Rinehart and Winston, 1974.

Tinker, J.: Intermarriage and Ethnic Boundaries: the Japanese American Case. Paper presented at the Meeting of the Pacific Sociological Association, Portland, Oregon. 1972.

Tseng, W. et al. (Eds.): Adjustment in Intercultural Marriage. Honolulu, HI: University of Hawaii Press, 1977.

Urban Associates.: A study of selected Socio-Economic Characteristics of Ethnic Minorities Based on the 1970 Census. Vol. 2 Asian Americans. Washington, D.C.: Government Printing Office, 1974.

U.S. Bureau of Census Perspectives on American Husbands and Wives. Current Population Reports, Series p. 23, No. 77. Washington, D.C.: Government Printing Office, 1978.

U.S. Bureau of the Census. Statistical Abstract of the United States. Washington, D.C.: Government Printing Office, 1981.

Vontress, C.: Racial and Ethnic Barriers in Counseling. In P. Pederson et al. (Eds.): Counseling Across Cultures. Honolulu, HI: University Press of Hawaii, 1976.

Wachtel, S.: To Think About the Unthinkable, Social Casework, 51: 467–474, 1978.

Wagner, R.: Changes in the Friend Network During the First Year of Single Parenthood for Mexican American and Anglo Women. In C. Everett (Ed.): Minority and Ethnic Issues in the Divorce Process. New York: Haworth, 1988.

Watzlawick, P. et al.: Change: Principles of Problem Formation and Resolution. New York: W. W. Norton, 1974.

Weiss, R.: Going it alone. New York: Basic Books, 1979.

Wetzel, C. and Wright, W.: Reciprocity of Therapist's Self-disclosure: Effects of Therapist's Race on Black Client's Disclosure—Paper presented at the Annual Meeting of the American Psychological Association, 1983.

Whitaker, C. and Keith, D.: Symbolic Experiential Family Therapy. In A. Gurman, and D. Kniskern (Eds.): Handbook of Family Therapy. New York: Brunner/Mazel, 1981.

Williams, T.: Substance Misuse and Alcoholism in the Military Family. In F. Kaslow and R. Ridenour (Eds.). The Military Family. New York: Guifford Press, 1984.

Wynne, L. The Epigenesis of Relational Systems: A Model for Understanding Family Development. Family Process, 23: 297–318, 1984.

AUTHOR INDEX

133

SUBJECT INDEX